Hawai'i's Favorite

PINEAPPLE

Recipes

A special Mahalo to:

Aloha Nursing & Rehab Centre for allowing
us to use their facilities.

Chef Grace Kusuhara for her assistance
in testing recipes.

A plantation manager squeezes a
freshly picked pineapple to test its ripeness,
while field workers scan the rows for mature
fruit. Pineapples are generally harvested
at maximum ripeness, but should be
firm to the touch.

Hawai'i's Favorite
PINEAPPLE
Recipes

Recipes by
Joannie Dobbs, Ph.D., C.N.S.
Text by
Betty Shimabukuro

Photography by
Ray Wong

Food preparation & styling by
Chef David Koerner, CC, C.D.M.
Drink preparation & styling by
Deborah Goldberg

Mutual Publishing

Library of Congress Catalog Card
Number: 2002109111

ISBN 1-56647-566-X

Art direction and design by Jane Hopkins

Third Printing (Dole) November 2006
3 4 5 6 7 8 9

Mutual Publishing
1215 Center Street, Suite 210
Honolulu, Hawai'i 96816
Ph: (808) 732-1709
Fax: (808) 734-4094
e-mail: info@mutualpublishing.com
www.mutualpublishing.com

Printed in Korea

TABLE of CONTENTS

A female pineapple picker removes the crowns before stacking the fruit in crates to be transported to the cannery. Although most of the early pineapple field workers were men, a handful of women toiled under the hot sun on plantations.

SALSAS · 43

SWEET, SOUR, & SAVORY · 53

SIMPLY SAVORY · 73

ON THE SIDE · 93

During the late nineteenth and early twentieth centuries, immigrant laborers from Portugal, Asia, the Philippines and the South Pacific came to Hawai'i as contract workers for island plantations. They would carefully pluck ripe fruit from the prickly plants while a plantation foreman, or luna, supervised on horseback.

DESSERTS · 107

95 Pineapples at Harvest Time - Hawaiian Islands

The workforce on pineapple plantations was comprised mostly of Japanese, Okinawan, and Filipino immigrant laborers. After their contracts were fulfilled, many set down roots in Hawai'i rather than return to uncertain futures in their homelands.

Above: An old advertisement from 1926.
Following page, top: Pineapples were first commercialized in Hawaiʻi in the early 1850s. An early plantation manager surveys a field of nearly ripe fruit. **Bottom:** In the early twentieth century, visitors to the Islands could buy fresh Hawaiian pineapples at stands along the main highways on Maui, Oʻahu and Kauaʻi. Here, a Hawaiian Pineapple Company employee selects the best fruits for a couple of well-to-do ladies.

INTRODUCTION

IF THE STATE of Hawai'i were to get a tattoo, it would be in the image of a pineapple. More photogenic than a coconut, more palatable than poi, the pineapple has grown into the universal symbol of these islands.

Yet the pineapple is a non-native. Hawaiians called it *hala* kahiki—*hala* after the prickly fruit of the hala tree, also called pandanus or screw pine; *kahiki* meaning "foreign country."

The fruit hails from South America and likely ended up on the Island of Hawai'i in the sixteenth century, following the shipwreck of a Spanish vessel carrying goods from Mexico. A small, fibrous and highly acidic variety eventually took root, and became known as the Wild Kailua.

In 1882, James Kidwell, an English horticulturist and retired sea captain, began experimenting with several varieties of pineapple in Mānoa, on land that eventually became the University of Hawai'i's flagship campus. The Smooth Cayenne prevailed, and continues to be the primary variety grown commercially. Kidwell was never commercially successful, but his contributions earned him the title, "Father of the Pineapple."

Most of the pineapple trade before the turn of the century involved fresh pineapple, which suffered a high rate of spoilage when shipped. But early canned products were so unstable that cans would occasionally explode. Plus, the United States collected a prohibitively high tariff on canned pineapple.

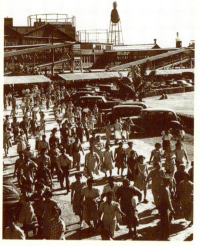

With annexation, however, came the end of the tariffs and pineapple got its chance. In 1901, James Dole, a young man with a degree in business and $1,000 to spend, formed Hawaiian Pineapple Co. (now Dole Food Co.). In 1906, he built a cannery in Iwilei. With its 100,000-gallon pineapple-shaped water tank on the roof, the cannery became a landmark and grew into the largest in world.

The industry spread to Maui, Hawai'i, Kaua'i and, of course, Lāna'i. Dole purchased most of Lāna'i in 1922, turning it into a mega-plantation.

By 1950, more than half of the world's pineapple came from Hawai'i.

Hundreds of Dole employees depart from the Iwilei Cannery after a long day of work. The 100,000-gallon pineapple-shaped water tank on the cannery roof, designed in 1927, became an icon that symbolized Hawai'i to millions of visitors.

The harvesting machine shown here sped up the picking process by providing field workers with a conveyor belt to transport pineapples to the truck. Other technological advances on the plantations, such as drip irrigation and paper mulching, allowed companies like Dole to increase production over the years.

For years, pineapple and sugar were Hawai'i's leading industries, only to suffer twin fates. The development of farming in countries with lower production costs—Mexico, Thailand, and the Philippines, primarily—cost the State its competitive edge.

Pineapple slips, suckers and crowns harvested from mature plants are used as propagating material to begin a new crop. Approximately one year after planting, the pineapple "bud" forms, and several months later the pineapple is ready to be harvested.

Hawai'i now produces less than 15 percent of the world's supply of pineapple. Lana'i has been transformed from the Pineapple Island into a luxury resort. The Dole water tower has been dismantled and the cannery turned into a shopping/entertainment complex; Dole's North Shore plantation is now a tourist attraction featuring the world's largest maze.

The industry perseveres, however. Development of lower-acid varieties continues, with Sugarloaf, Hawaiian Gold, white and organic pineapples gaining footholds in

restaurants and specialty markets. Processed foods bearing local labels—such as pineapple sauces, salsas and drinks—also guarantee that the prickly pine will continue to be associated with the islands of Hawai'i.

The field sprayer, shown here, was developed on the "Pineapple Isle" of Lāna'i in the 1950s. Today, it is still used to water young pineapple starts and to supply growing plants with nutrients like nitrogen, iron and zinc.

PINEAPPLE USES

The Pineapple

ENDS
SHELL
CORE
TRIMMINGS

converted into sugar — residue is manufactured into stock food, alcohol, etc.

SHELL EXTRACT

"EXTRA QUALITY" "STANDARD QUALITY" "BROKEN SLICES"

Due to irregular and badly broken pieces, this is crushed and combined with shell extraction.

Sliced Hawaiian Pineapple   Crushed Hawaiian Pineapp

Hawaiian pineapples were commercially canned for the first time in 1882. In the beginning, difficulty acquiring cans and high tariffs on processed food products shipped from Hawai'i to the U.S. made canning pineapple unprofitable. After Hawai'i became an American territory in 1898, however, tariffs on Hawaiian exports were lifted, and the canned pineapple industry took off. This early diagram demonstrates the breakdown of how pineapple parts were used in the canning process.

THE PINEAPPLE IS a formidable fruit, armor-plated and prickly. It can seem impenetrable on first approach. There's gold inside, though, so breaking in is worth the struggle.

In the Caribbean, where Christopher Columbus "discovered" the pineapple in 1493, the juice was used to soften skin and heal wounds. Spanish explorers ate pineapples to prevent scurvy. Along with vitamin C, the fruit also contains high quantities of the Bromelain enzyme, a digestive aid and an anti-inflammatory.

Pineapples do not sweeten once picked; therefore, they must be harvested ripe. To select one, don't go by color. A ripe fruit may still be mottled green and brown. It should have a deep, sweet scent and give off a solid thud when flicked. Pick one that is slightly soft, with a compact crown.

If the pineapple is kept a few days before eating, its acids will mellow, but the fruit will not get any more ripe or sweet.

Packers carefully inspected the pineapple slices, sorting them into grades of "fancy," "choice," "broken slices," and "tidbits," then placed them in the appropriate cans.

To trim, take a very sharp knife and cut off the crown. Then cut a slice off the bottom so it will stand firm. Cut off the skin in thin slices from top to bottom. The fibrous eyes will remain; cut them out in diagonal grooves, spiraling around the fruit. The fruit can then be cut into wedges, round slices or chunks. Don't cut off the core; it can be the sweetest part.

Another method is to quarter the fruit, then slice off the skin, piece-by-piece. Fresh pineapple may also be purchased pre-cut.

Canned pineapple is available packed in unsweetened juice or in syrup. Read recipes carefully to see which is needed; results will vary greatly.

Fresh pineapple may be pickled or turned into jam. To can, simmer 10 minutes in water, sugar syrup, apple or fruit juice, then fill jars and process.

To freeze, pack fruit tightly into a container with 1/2-inch space on top. If desired, sweeten with a syrup made from equal parts water and sugar. Crushed fruit and juice (unsweetened or with granulated sugar added) may also be frozen.

Pineapple growers have been experimenting with different varieties and growing techniques since the early 1900s. Beginning in 1925, laboratory scientists tested innovative methods of fertilizing, planting, cloning, and controlling insects and plant diseases among pineapples at the Experiment Station located at the University of Hawai'i.

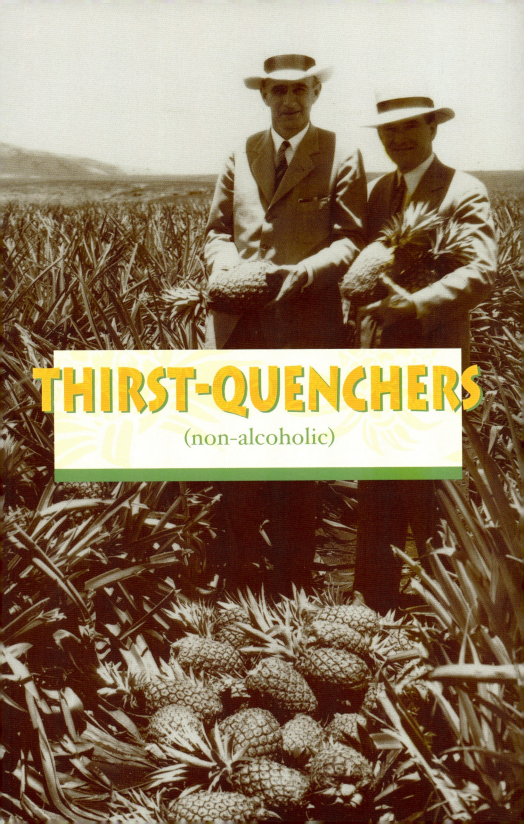

THIRST-QUENCHERS

(non-alcoholic)

PINEAPPLE IS AMONG THE
JUICIEST OF FRUITS, WITH A FLAVOR
PROFILE MADE FOR REFRESHING DRINKS.
PINEAPPLE IS A STANDARD INGREDIENT IN
TROPICAL DRINKS SUCH AS THE PIÑA COLADA
AND BLUE HAWAII, BUT IT DOESN'T TAKE
ALCOHOL TO MAKE A GREAT PINEAPPLE
DRINK. THE TARTNESS OF PINEAPPLE PAIRS
WELL WITH SWEETER FLAVORS SUCH AS
ORANGE OR BERRY, WITH THE SPARKLE OF
CLUB SODA OR THE CREAMINESS
OF ICE CREAM.

SIMPLY ADD ICE AND STIR.

Previous page: James Dole (shown at left),
founder of the Dole Foods Company, started out with a 61-acre plot
of land in Wahiawā, Oʻahu that he bought in 1900 for $4,000. Today,
his name is one of the best-known food brands in the world,
alongside corporate giants such as Kraft and Coca-Cola.

SIMPLY PINEAPPLE PUNCH

Serves 2 (2-1/2 cups punch)

It can't get any easier than pouring a few juices together to make a tall, refreshing drink. Don't forget the mint— it adds the crisp scent of freshness.

1/2 cup chilled pineapple juice
1/2 cup chilled orange juice
1/2 cup chilled cranberry juice
1/2 cup chilled club soda
1/2 cup chilled Simple Sweet and Sour Mix (See recipe on page 21)
Ice

Garnish: Mint leaves

Fill two 16-ounce glasses with ice.

Combine ingredients in a large pitcher, or pour directly on the rocks and stir.

Garnish with one or two mint leaves each.

This can also be made by combining ingredients and ice in a blender.

HAWAIIAN SUNRISE

Serves 4 (4 cups)

The colors of the sky at dawn distinguish
this creamy pick-me-up.

1-1/2 cups fresh or canned crushed pineapple
1/2 cup vanilla ice cream
1-1/2 cups fresh orange juice
Juice from 1 lime
1 cup ice cubes
Dash of maraschino cherry juice

   In a blender, combine crushed pineapple, vanilla ice cream, orange and lime juices; cover and blend until smooth.
   With blender running, gradually add ice cubes and blend until smooth.
   Pour into two tall glasses and drizzle maraschino cherry juice on top to splash a bit of sun.

TROPICAL FRUIT PUNCH

Makes about 1-1/2 quarts (6 cups)

*A mini-iceberg of frozen molded sugar cools
down this punch, while dressing it up for a party.*

1 cup water

2/3 cup granulated sugar

2 cups ginger ale

1 cup club soda

1 cup pineapple juice

2 tablespoons frozen orange juice concentrate, thawed

1 banana

1-1/3 tablespoons fresh lemon juice

Garnish: Orange and Lemon slices

In a small nonreactive (stainless) pan, combine sugar and water and boil to dissolve. Set aside and cool. Pour into a mold and freeze. The mold must fit into the punch bowl and be as decorative as possible. A fluted shallow gelatin mold is ideal.

About 45 minutes before serving, place the frozen molded sugar solution in the punch bowl and pour half of the ginger ale and club soda over frozen mixture.

Combine fruit juices and banana in a blender and pulse until smooth. Pour into the punch bowl. Stir and add remaining ginger ale and club soda. Stir again. Garnish and serve.

PINEAPPLE COOLER

Serves 2 (about 1 cup)

Think of the pineapple sticks in this drink as more than a garnish. Once they soak up the sweet, sparkling brew, chew them slowly—it's like dessert.

4 ounces pineapple juice

1 teaspoon granulated sugar

4 ounces lemon soda

Crushed ice

Garnish: Pineapple sticks (see Note)

Stir sugar into pineapple juice until dissolved.

Fill two wide-mouthed glasses with ice. Pour pineapple mixture and then top with lemon soda.

Garnish each glass with a fresh pineapple stick.

NOTE: Cut a fresh pineapple near the core into 4 to 6-inch sticks.

PINEAPPLE ICE CREAM SHAKE

Serves 3 (about 6 cups)

Forget chocolate. A pineapple shake is a great change of pace, with a full-flavor boost.

2 cups crushed pineapple packed in heavy syrup
2 cups vanilla ice cream
1/4 cup lemon juice
2 cups ice cubes

Combine crushed pineapple, ice cream and lemon juice in a blender and blend well.

Gradually add ice cubes and blend until smooth. Pour into wide-mouthed glasses.

To prepare ahead of time, pour into glasses and refrigerate. Mixture will stay thick and creamy in the refrigerator.

HAWAIIAN FRUIT PUNCH

Serves 2 (about 2 cups)

*Guava and passion fruit combine with pineapple
to create a taste of aloha.*

2 ounces fresh lemon juice
Juice of a small lime
2 ounces guava nectar
2 ounces pineapple juice
2 ounces passion fruit juice drink
1 ounce maraschino cherry juice
Club soda to fill
Crushed ice

In a pitcher, combine fruit juice ingredients and stir.
Fill two chimney glasses with crushed ice and pour in fruit juice mixture. Top with club soda and stir.

PINEAPPLE BERRY YOGURT SHAKE

Banana and berries are a classic pairing in smoothies, but add pineapple and your drink takes on tropical appeal.

1 cup berry yogurt
1 small banana
1 cup fresh or frozen berries (reserve 3 whole berries for garnish)
1 cup canned crushed pineapple with juice
2 tablespoons lemon juice
2 cups ice cubes
2 teaspoons granulated sugar (optional)

Combine yogurt, cut-up banana, berries, pineapple with its juice, and lemon juice in a blender; cover blender and pulse-blend about 15 seconds.

With blender running, gradually add ice cubes, blending until smooth.

Top off with a berry if desired. Serve immediately.

SOFT PIÑA COLADA

Serves 2 (about 1 cup)

For coconut lovers, this drink will prove irresistible.

1/2 cup crushed pineapple in heavy syrup
1/4 cup coconut cream
4 ice cubes

Garnish: Pineapple stick rolled in granulated sugar (see Note, page 7).

Combine pineapple, syrup, and coconut cream in a blender. Pulse a few seconds. Add ice cubes and blend well.

Pour into two wide-mouthed glasses. Serve with a sugared pineapple stick.

HOT WASSAIL

Serves 8 (8 cups)

This is a perfect holiday drink, fragrant with the scents of cinnamon, nutmeg and cloves.

4 cups unsweetened apple juice
3 cups unsweetened pineapple juice
1 cup cranberry juice cocktail
1/4 teaspoon ground nutmeg
1 cinnamon stick
3 whole cloves

Garnish: Lemon slices

Combine ingredients, except lemon slices, in a pot and simmer for about 10 minutes.

Strain into mugs, top with lemon slice and serve hot.

THIRST-QUENCHERS

(alcoholic)

BLUE HAWAII

Serves 1 (about 1 cup)

A classic drink that conjures memories of Elvis.

1-1/2 ounces vodka or light rum
3/4 ounce blue curacao
1-1/2 ounces pineapple juice
1 ounce Simple Sweet and Sour Mix (see recipe on page 21)

Combine ingredients in a blender with a scoop of crushed ice. Blend for about 15 to 20 seconds.
Pour into a 14-ounce Collins glass.

PIÑA COLADA

Serves 2 (about 1/2 cup)

So rich and creamy, a Piña Colada is like drinking your dessert.

2 ounces coconut cream
4 ounces pineapple juice
2 ounces light rum
2 cups crushed ice

Garnish: cherry and pineapple stick

Combine ingredients in a blender with a scoop of crushed ice. Blend for about 15 to 20 seconds.
Pour into a 14-ounce Collins glass and serve with a straw.

Previous page: This early twentieth-century postcard captures the agricultural past of windward Oʻahu. Before 1928, pineapple fields stretched all the way from inland Kāneʻohe to the bay, an area now covered by housing developments and Kamehameha Highway.

HAWAIIAN WINE COOLER

Serves 6 (about 6 cups)

*When the party's over, the citrus wheels used
to garnish this punch bowl are great to suck on.*

1 lemon

1 orange

2 tablespoons granulated sugar

2 cups chilled pineapple juice

2 cups chilled dry white wine

1-1/2 cups chilled sparkling water

Garnish: Wheels of oranges, lemons, or limes

Slice orange and lemon in half. Cut 2 or 3 thin slices of fruit from centers of each citrus. Place slices in a 2- to 3-quart pitcher. From the remaining fruit ends, squeeze juice through a strainer into the pitcher.

Combine sugar and pineapple juice and stir to dissolve the sugar. Add to the pitcher along with white wine and sparkling water. Stir.

Serve wine cooler over crushed ice in stemmed glasses or in a punch bowl. Garnish and serve.

Hawai'i's Favorite Pineapple Recipes

SANGRIA FRUIT PUNCH

Serves 8 (about 6 cups)

Burgundy gives this mix of juices real depth of flavor.

1-1/2 cups frozen raspberries or strawberries
1 (750-ml) bottle burgundy wine
1/3 cup pineapple juice
1/3 cup apple juice
1/3 cup orange juice
1/3 cup cranberry juice
Chilled black cherry soda to taste
Crushed ice

In a blender, pulse berries and wine and pour into a 2- to 3-quart pitcher. Stir in remaining fruit juice and chill thoroughly.

To serve, add ice to each glass and pour 1 cup of wine blend with one scoop of ice. Top off with black cherry soda and stir.

Enjoy.

FROSTY PINEAPPLE MARGARITA

Serves 1 (about 3/4 cup)

Pineapple gives this traditional drink a tropical twist.

1 lime wedge for coating rim of glass
Kosher salt for coating rim of glass
1-1/4 ounces tequila
2 ounces Sweet & Sour Margarita Mix (see recipe
   on page 22)
1/8 cup crushed pineapple
1/2 ounce Simple Syrup (see recipe on page 21)
5 ice cubes

Rub the rim of a margarita glass with a lime wedge and dip the rim in kosher salt to lightly coat. Chill the glass.

In a blender, blend remaining ingredients, including ice cubes, for 30 seconds. Pour slurry into a chilled glass and serve.

PINEAPPLE PUNCH

Serves 1 (about 1 cup)

Sweet-sour flavors mellow the bite of the rums in this fruity cocktail.

1 ounce light rum
1/2 ounce dark rum
3 ounces freshly squeezed orange juice
2 ounces pineapple juice
1/4 cup Simple Sweet and Sour Mix (see recipe on page 21)
Splash of grenadine (optional)
Squeeze of lemon
Crushed ice

Garnish: Orange wedge and a Cherry

Mix all ingredients together and shake. In a tall glass, serve over crushed ice and garnish with a wedge of citrus and a cherry.

Plantation laborers were housed in "camps" clustered near the fields and canneries. This housing camp was built by the Hawaiian Pineapple Company for workers on "The Pineapple Island" of Lāna'i.

Hawai'i's Favorite Pineapple Recipes

SIMPLE SYRUP

Makes 5 cups

Make up a quantity of these mixers and you'll be able to tend bar all night.

2 cups granulated sugar
5 cups water

In a large saucepan, combine water and sugar and stir over medium heat until sugar dissolves. Bring to a simmer and then cool.

SIMPLE SWEET AND SOUR MIX

Makes 1/4 cup

1/4 cup fresh lemon juice
1/4 cup granulated sugar

In a small saucepan, combine lemon juice and sugar and stir over medium heat until sugar dissolves. Remove from heat and cool.

2 1/4 Cups EACH

use = 18 oz

SWEET AND SOUR MARGARITA MIX

Makes about 7 cups

3 cups water
3 cups granulated sugar
2 cups fresh lemon juice
2 cups fresh lime juice

In a large saucepan, combine water and sugar and stir over medium heat until sugar dissolves. Bring to a simmer and then cool.

Mix syrup, lemon juice and lime juice in a pitcher. Chill until cold. (Can be made one week ahead. Cover and keep chilled.)

SALADS & DIPS

LET GO OF THE IDEA OF
A TYPICAL FRUIT SALAD BUILT ON
SWEETNESS. PINEAPPLE ADDS TARTNESS
AND A GOLDEN GLOW TO THE USUAL APPLES
AND BANANAS OF A FRUIT BOWL. IT ALSO
LENDS ITSELF WELL TO SAVORY SALADS, SUCH
AS COLESLAW, THAT WOULD BE REFRESHING
SIDE DISHES SERVED WITH BURGERS OR
BARBECUE.

PINEAPPLE HONEYDEW SALAD WITH HONEY MUSTARD DRESSING

Serves 4

*Mustard and sweet onions punch up
a mix of melons and pineapple.*

Prepare Honey Mustard Dressing (see recipe on page 26)
6 cups mixed baby salad greens
1 cucumber
2 cups fresh pineapple cubes or wedges
2 cups honeydew melon cut into 1/2-inch slices

Wash and towel-dry greens and cucumber. Slice cucumbers on a diagonal. Refrigerate until ready to serve.

Cut fruit and refrigerate until ready to serve.

To serve: Place greens on bottom of four large-mouth salad bowls and top with pineapple, honeydew melon and cucumber. Drizzle with Honey Mustard Dressing.

HONEY MUSTARD DRESSING

Makes about 1/2 cup

1/4 cup pineapple juice

2 tablespoons honey mustard

1 tablespoon fresh lime juice

1/4 cup minced **Maui** or **Ewa** onion

1 tablespoon minced fresh mint

1/4 teaspoon **Kosher** salt

1/8 teaspoon course black pepper

In small bowl, whisk together pineapple juice, mustard, lime juice, onion, mint, salt and pepper. Cover and refrigerate for 1 hour.

CLASSIC LIME PINEAPPLE MOLD

Serves 8

This is the classic layered salad Mom used to make for the holidays, but it's a refresher year-round.

1 (3-ounce) package lime gelatin
1 cup boiling water
1 cup canned crushed pineapple in heavy syrup
1 cup creamed cottage cheese
1/4 cup chopped walnuts

Stir boiling water into gelatin until completely dissolved (at least 2 minutes). Fold in pineapple and syrup, cottage cheese, and walnuts and mix until evenly distributed. Pour into a single ring mold or into individual serving molds and chill overnight, or until firm.

Set at room temperature for 5 minutes and then unmold on to freshly rinsed lettuce leaves.

TROPICAL MIXED FRUIT SALAD

Serves 4

The combination of fruit and spice here
makes for a salad with bite.

2 tablespoons honey
1/4 cup Cream Salad Dressing (see recipe on page 30)
1/4 cup Hot Pepper Dressing (see recipe on page 30)
1 cup crushed pineapple
1 cup sliced banana
1 cup diced papaya
1 cup melon pieces (1/2-inch cubes)
Lettuce
Cayenne pepper or nutmeg to taste

Combine honey and dressings and let flavors infuse for about 1 hour in the refrigerator.

Toss together fruit and arrange on lettuce and sprinkle with a little cayenne pepper or a little grated nutmeg.

CREAM SALAD DRESSING

Makes about 1/3 cup

1/4 cup heavy whipping cream
1/8 teaspoon kosher salt
1 teaspoon granulated sugar
Pinch of black pepper
1 tablespoon white cider vinegar

Beat cream until it thickens.
Stir in salt, sugar, and pepper and mix well.
Slowly add and beat in the vinegar. Refrigerate.

HOT PEPPER DRESSING

Makes about 1/3 cup

2 tablespoons olive oil
1/2 teaspoon salt
1/4 teaspoon cayenne pepper
1/8 teaspoon granulated sugar
2 tablespoons white cider vinegar

Place ingredients in a small jar, cover tightly, and chill thoroughly in the refrigerator.
Shake vigorously for 1 to 2 minutes, just before serving.

PINEAPPLE CABBAGE SALAD

Serves 4

Think of this as a tropical coleslaw and take it on a
picnic, along with your hibachi-grilled chicken and meats.

3 cups shredded cabbage
1 cup grated carrots
1 cup crushed pineapple
1/8 cup packed raisins
2 tablespoons mayonnaise
1/4 tablespoon Japanese rice vinegar
1/2 teaspoon fresh lime juice
1/8 teaspoon finely minced Hawaiian chili pepper
Salt and pepper to taste

Garnish: Chopped peanuts

In a large bowl, combine cabbage, carrots, pineapple, and raisins. Set aside.

In a cup, combine mayonnaise, rice vinegar, lime juice, and chili pepper. Toss with salad and serve with a garnish of chopped peanuts.

WARM PINEAPPLE SPINACH SALAD

Serves 4

*Mandarin oranges are the usual fruit of choice
in spinach salads, but pineapple is a great change of pace.*

Pineapple Dressing (see recipe below)
1 pound spinach leaves
2 cups button mushrooms
1 cup diced pineapple

**Garnish: Chopped macadamia nuts or minced cooked
   bacon**

Blend Pineapple Dressing and set aside to simmer until just before serving.

Clean all vegetables and slice mushrooms.

In a large serving bowl, toss vegetables and diced pineapple with the freshly made warm dressing.

Place on salad plates and sprinkle with macadamia nuts or bits of bacon.

PINEAPPLE DRESSING

Makes about 1 cup

3/4 cup pineapple juice
2 tablespoons champagne vinegar
1/4 cup diced pineapple
1/2 teaspoon kosher salt

Combine all dressing ingredients in a blender and pulse-blend until smooth. Just before serving, pour into a saucepan and heat until it simmers.

Hawai'i's Favorite Pineapple Recipes

PINEAPPLE CARROT SALAD

Serves 4

Grated carrots and yogurt go into this creamy mix,
an alternative to coleslaw.

1 cup crushed pineapple, drained
1/4 cup packed raisins
1/2 cup plain yogurt
2 tablespoons fresh lemon juice
1 tablespoon honey
4 cups grated carrots

Garnish: 1/4 cup chopped walnuts

In a large bowl, combine pineapple, raisins, yogurt, lemon juice, and honey, and toss.

Fold in carrots. Cover bowl and refrigerate overnight.

Portion onto salad plates and garnish with walnuts.

POPPYSEED DRESSING

Makes about 1/2 cup

1/4 cup mayonnaise
1/4 cup sour cream
1-1/2 tablespoons honey
2 scant teaspoons distilled white vinegar
1-1/4 teaspoons poppy seeds

In a small bowl, combine ingredients. Whisk together until smooth. Cover and refrigerate overnight to allow the flavors to infuse.

PINEAPPLE SLAW WITH FETA CHEESE

Serves 4

*For those who prefer their slaws without mayonnaise,
here's a tangy alternative.*

1 cup minced fresh (or canned) pineapple

2 cups shredded carrot

1 green pepper, julienned

3 tablespoons white wine vinegar

3 tablespoons pineapple juice

1 tablespoon honey

1 teaspoon canola oil

8 tablespoons crumbled feta cheese or 4 tablespoons each
   feta and blue cheese

In a large bowl, toss together pineapple, carrot, and green pepper.
Set aside.

In a small bowl, whisk together vinegar, pineapple juice, honey,
and canola oil. Pour over slaw mixture and toss. Cover and chill 1
hour. Top with feta and blue cheese just before serving.

PINEAPPLE CHICKEN SALAD

Makes 4 salad appetizers or 2 main servings

*Macadamia nuts, olives and strips of chicken make
this a salad hearty enough to be a meal in itself.*

2 (6-ounce) skinless, boneless chicken breasts

2 teaspoons olive oil

1 cup pineapple cubes

1/2 cup diced celery

2 tablespoons minced Maui onion

4 large pitted black olives, minced

1/4 cup regular or low-fat Ranch dressing

8 leaves butterhead or any bibb lettuce

2 tablespoons chopped macadamia nuts

Rinse and dry chicken breasts. Slice into bite-size strips of about 1/2-inch thick and place in a small bowl. Toss with olive oil. Heat small skillet to hot and sear chicken about 30 to 45 seconds on each side (until pink is just gone). Remove to a plate. Add onion to the skillet and heat until the onions are translucent.

In a large bowl, toss pineapple, chicken, celery, onion and minced olives together. Dab Ranch dressing over top of salad and toss again.

Rinse lettuce leaves and pat dry.

For appetizer, arrange two leaves per plate and top with pineapple-chicken mixture. Sprinkle with macadamia nuts and serve. Use four lettuce leaves for main dish serving.

CURRIED PINEAPPLE TURKEY SALAD

Serves 4

A great way to finish off leftover turkey—your family won't even recognize it as leftovers.

2 cups cold cooked rice

1 cup diced cooked turkey

1/2 cup sliced celery

1/4 cup diced green bell pepper

1/2 cup canned pineapple chunks, drained

1/2 cup mayonnaise

2 teaspoons curry powder

1/8 teaspoon kosher salt

1/8 teaspoon ground ginger

8 red leaf lettuce leaves

Garnish: Chopped and seeded Roma tomato

In a large bowl, combine cooked rice, turkey, celery, bell pepper and pineapple chunks. Toss.

In a small bowl, whisk together mayonnaise, curry powder, salt and ginger. Add to turkey mixture and mix thoroughly. Cover and refrigerate 2 to 3 hours, or overnight.

Just before serving, wash lettuce and place on salad plates. Spoon turkey mixture onto salad greens and garnish with chopped tomato.

PINEAPPLE CRAB SALAD

Serves 4

This creamy mix would also make a nice dip for crackers or a sandwich filling for a nice French roll.

2 cups chunk crab meat

1/2 cup mayonnaise

1 teaspoon Worcestershire sauce

2 to 3 teaspoons Old Bay Spice

1 tablespoon ketchup

2 cups diced fresh pineapple or well-drained canned pineapple

2 Roma tomatoes, seeded and diced

Kosher salt and pepper to taste or approximately 1/8 teaspoon each

12 Manoa lettuce leaves or other bibb lettuce

In a medium bowl, combine crab, mayonnaise, Worcestershire, Old Bay Spice and ketchup. Once thoroughly mixed, add pineapple and toss.

To serve: Place three lettuce leaves per plate and top with a mound of crab mixture. Sprinkle with diced tomatoes and salt and black pepper to taste.

SOUTHERN PINEAPPLE BEAN SALAD

Serves 4

This mix of beans, peppers and fruit would be a distinctive contribution to a barbecue potluck.

1 (15-ounce) can black-eyed peas
1/3 cup minced celery
1/3 cup minced red onion
1/4 cup chopped roasted bell peppers
1 cup diced fresh pineapple
1 jalapeño chili pepper, seeded and minced
1 tablespoon Dijon mustard
2 tablespoons olive oil
2 teaspoons cider vinegar
1/4 teaspoon each of kosher salt and pepper
8 leaf lettuce leaves

Garnish: 2 tablespoons minced fresh cilantro

Rinse and drain black-eyed peas, repeat twice and place into a large bowl.

Add celery, red onion, bell peppers, pineapple, and jalapeño chili pepper and toss.

In a small bowl, mix together Dijon mustard, olive oil, and cider vinegar. Add to bean salad and toss until salad ingredients are coated with dressing. Cover and refrigerate until chilled.

To serve, place two leaf lettuce leaves on a salad plate and top with bean salad. Sprinkle with fresh cilantro.

SAVORY PINEAPPLE DIP

Makes about 2 cups

*Put this out for pre-dinner nibbling, but be careful
that your guests don't fill up on it!*

1/2 cup grated pineapple

1 package instant onion soup mix

1/4 cup minced cooked ham

4 ounces cream cheese, softened

1/2 cup heavy whipping cream

In a small bowl, combine pineapple, onion soup mix, and ham and mix thoroughly. Combine cream cheese and whipping cream and then fold into pineapple mixture. Cover and refrigerate for least 1 hour.

Serve with chips, crackers, or freshly prepared raw vegetables.

This early twentieth-century postcard is a humorous take on the arduous task of hauling pineapples by ox and cart.

HOT PINEAPPLE
DIPPING SAUCE

Makes about 3/4 cup sauce

Particularly good served with savory meats, poultry or seafood.

1 cup crushed pineapple in heavy syrup

2 tablespoons light corn syrup

1 tablespoon white vinegar

1 teaspoon grated lime zest

1/2 teaspoon grated fresh ginger

1/8 teaspoon crushed red pepper

1/4 teaspoon salt or to taste

In a blender, combine pineapple, corn syrup, vinegar, lime zest, ginger, and crushed red pepper. Cover and pulse-blend for about 15 seconds. Pour into a small non-reactive saucepan and bring sauce to a boil over medium-high heat; stir frequently to prevent burning. Reduce heat to simmer until thick (about 10 minutes).

SALSAS

PINEAPPLES ARE AN INTERNATIONAL SYMBOL OF HOSPITALITY. FOR GENERATIONS, THE GOLDEN FRUIT WITH ITS EMERALD CROWN HAS BEEN USED TO ORNAMENT HOMES AND PUBLIC BUILDINGS, WOVEN INTO WELCOME MATS, CARVED INTO DOORS, STENCILED ONTO FURNITURE.

THIS GIVES THE PINEAPPLE A LITTLE HIDDEN SIGNIFICANCE WHEN USED IN A DISH TO WELCOME GUESTS INTO YOUR HOME, SUCH AS A COLORFUL, REFRESHING BOWL OF SALSA.

Previous page: Early pineapple growers, including James Dole, started out living alone in tiny shacks among their pineapple plants. They plowed and planted their fields by hand with only a horse and wagon to help them. In 1900, Dole started out with a 61-acre plot of land covered with wild grass and guava trees. He built his multi-million dollar pineapple company from the ground up.

ROASTED PINEAPPLE MANGO SALSA

Makes about 3 cups

Roasting brings out the natural sweetness of pineapple which matches nicely with the mango and contrasts with the peppery bells.

1 cup diced roasted pineapple (see Note)
1/4 cup raisins
1 cup diced mango
1/4 cup diced red onion
1/2 small red bell pepper, sliced into 1/2-inch lengths
1/2 small green bell pepper, sliced into 1/2 -inch lengths
1 red chili pepper without seeds, minced
2 tablespoons lime juice
1/8 teaspoon salt
1 teaspoon granulated sugar

Prepare roasted pineapple. Set aside.

Place raisins and water in a small saucepan and simmer until raisins are plumped. Drain and set aside.

In a mixing bowl, combine roasted pineapple, mango, onion, bell peppers, chili pepper, and lime juice; mix together.

Season with salt and sugar and mix again. Cover and refrigerate overnight and use within three days.

NOTE: Preheat oven to 350 degrees Fahrenheit. Remove pineapple skin and slice lengthwise—approximately 1/4-inch thick. Spread out on a sheet pan and bake for approximately 20 to 25 minutes, or until the pineapple releases its liquid. Remove pineapple center core and dice. Refrigerate until needed.

SIMPLE PINEAPPLE MANGO SALSA

Makes about 2 cups

Jerk seasoning is a staple of Caribbean cooking, used to make Jerk Chicken. Try this salsa alongside roast chicken or turkey.

I (14-ounce) can pineapple chunks in juice
I cup mango chutney (or any fruit chutney)
I to 2 teaspoons jerk seasoning (see Note)

Drain pineapple and combine pineapple with chutney. Add jerk seasoning a little at a time and pulse in a food processor until the desired consistency is reached. Do Not Purée.

Serve with taco or taro chips or chilled sliced cucumbers.

NOTE: Jerk seasonings vary greatly, add carefully.

TOTALLY TROPICAL FRUIT SALSA

Makes about 2 cups

Each scoop of this salsa is like a tiny fruit bowl.

1/4 cup minced fresh pineapple
1/4 cup minced papaya
1/4 cup minced mango
1/4 cup minced kiwi
1/4 cup minced red bell pepper
1/3 cup minced red onion
2 tablespoons minced red chili pepper
1/4 cup minced cilantro or mint (see **Note**)
2 tablespoons fresh lime juice
1/2 teaspoon kosher salt
1/8 teaspoon coarse black pepper

Clean fruit and vegetables, mince, and toss together in a medium mixing bowl. Season with lime juice and salt and pepper. Refrigerate until chilled.

NOTE: Cilantro and mint can be used together with the total equaling 1/4 cup minced herb.

PINEAPPLE GRAPEFRUIT SALSA

Makes about 4 cups

Plenty of tart, citrus flavors here,
but pepper and onions give it a savory slant.

1 small grapefruit

1 sweet orange

1 cup crushed pineapple in heavy syrup

1/2 cup diced red onion

1 small red bell pepper, seeded and diced

1 jalapeño pepper, seeded and diced

2 tablespoons sliced green onion tops

1/4 teaspoon kosher salt

1 teaspoon olive oil

Peel and segment grapefruit and orange and dice. Place in a medium bowl along with the pineapple, red onion, diced peppers, and green onion tops. Toss. Sprinkle with kosher salt and olive oil and toss again.

CONFETTI PINEAPPLE SALSA

Makes about 3 cups

*Cumin and coriander give this mix
a slight flavor of curry. Try it as a garnish
the next time you serve curry.*

2 cups diced fresh pineapple or well-drained, canned
   pineapple chunks
1/4 cup diced red onion
1/4 cup each diced green and yellow bell pepper
2 tablespoons chopped raisins
1 teaspoon minced garlic clove
1 jalapeño pepper, seeded and minced
1/2 teaspoon ground coriander
1/4 teaspoon ground cumin
1/8 teaspoon kosher salt

Garnish: 2 Roma tomatoes, seeded and diced

In a medium bowl, combine and fold together pineapple, onion, bell pepper, garlic, and raisins.

In a cup, combine jalapeño, coriander, cumin, and salt and sprinkle over pineapple mixture. Toss until spices are evenly distributed. Cover and refrigerate overnight.

Garnish with freshly diced tomatoes.

PINEAPPLE GINGER SALSA

Makes about 2 cups

Jalapeño and ginger both add heat, while lime juice adds tang to this rainbow of flavors.

1-1/2 cups chopped pineapple
1/2 cup diced red onion
1 minced jalapeño chili, seeded
1 tablespoon finely grated fresh ginger
Zest of 1 lime
1 tablespoon fresh lime juice
1/2 cup chopped cilantro or American parsley
Salt and pepper to taste

In a small bowl, combine pineapple, onion and jalapeño. Toss and add lime zest, lime juice and 3 tablespoons chopped cilantro. Toss again. Transfer to serving bowl and sprinkle with remaining 1 tablespoon cilantro.

Cover and refrigerate for a few hours to allow flavors to infuse.

SWEET, SOUR & SAVORY

SWEET-AND-SOUR DESCRIBES
A BALANCE BETWEEN SWEETNESS AND
STRONG, PUNGENT FLAVORS. THIS BALANCE IS
BROUGHT ABOUT BY THE INFUSION OF SUGAR
AND VINEGAR IN JUST THE RIGHT
PROPORTIONS.

THE ADDITION OF PINEAPPLE,
WITH ITS SWEET-SOUR FLAVOR AND
ACIDITY, IS A PERFECT CHOICE. PINEAPPLE IS
PARTICULARLY EXCELLENT IN SWEET-SOUR
MARINADES, NOT ONLY FOR ITS FLAVOR, BUT
ALSO BECAUSE IT CONTAINS AN ENZYME
THAT DIGESTS PROTEIN AND SERVES
AS A NATURAL TENDERIZER.

Previous page: The pineapple fields of central Oʻahu
are depicted in this photograph from the late 1930s. Photos of
Hawaiʻi's pineapple plantations were popular postcard images
among visitors during the early twentieth century.

TROPICAL SWEET AND SOUR MARINADE

Makes about 1 cup

Spike your barbecued meats with the heat of ginger in combination with the sweetness of pineapple.

3/4 cup pineapple syrup (drained from canned pineapple)

3 tablespoons Worcestershire sauce

1 tablespoon fresh ginger, minced

1 teaspoon salt

1 teaspoon garlic, peeled and minced

In a saucepan, combine all ingredients and bring to a simmer. Then brush over your favorite ribs, chicken or pork during the last 15 minutes of cooking.

BASIC SWEET AND SOUR SAUCES

The procedure for each of these sauce recipes is as easy as 1 - 2 - 3.

1. In a saucepan, combine all sauce ingredients.
2. Bring mixture to a boil, stirring until thick.
3. Use as a dip or pour over your entrée or vegetable.

BASIC SWEET AND SOUR PINEAPPLE SAUCE

Makes about 1-1/2 cups

2/3 cup heavy syrup from canned pineapple

1/3 cup cider vinegar

2 tablespoons water

1/4 cup soy sauce

1 tablespoon ketchup

2 tablespoons cornstarch

2 tablespoons granulated sugar

BASIC SWEET AND SOUR
PINEAPPLE SAUCE - TAKE 2

Makes about 2 cups

1 tablespoon cornstarch

2 teaspoons soy sauce

1/2 cup packed brown sugar

1/3 cup cider vinegar

1/2 cup pineapple syrup (syrup from pineapple chunks)

1 (20-ounce) can pineapple chunks

BASIC SWEET AND SOUR
PINEAPPLE SAUCE - TAKE 3

Makes about 3 cups

4 tablespoons packed brown sugar

2 tablespoons cornstarch

3/4 cup cider vinegar

1 tablespoon soy sauce

1-1/4 cups pineapple juice

1/4 teaspoon ground ginger

1 cup Russian dressing

VIETNAMESE SWEET AND SOUR SAUCE

Makes about 1 cup

*This pungent blend has tomatoes as its base,
but carries the exotic flavors of chili paste and fish sauce.*

2 shallots, minced

2 cloves garlic, minced

2 teaspoons canola oil

1/2 teaspoon ground chili paste

1 tablespoon ketchup

2 teaspoons fish sauce

2 teaspoons granulated sugar

1/2 cup chopped tomatoes

1/4 cup chicken stock or canned low-sodium chicken broth

1 tablespoon cornstarch

3 tablespoons water

1/4 teaspoon fresh lemon juice

In a saucepan over moderate heat, sauté shallots and garlic in oil until just golden. Mix in chili paste, ketchup, fish sauce, and sugar and stir for 1 minute. Add the tomatoes and chickenstock and cook over low heat until slightly reduced, about 3 to 5 minutes.

Stir water into cornstarch and add 1 teaspoon at a time to sauce, stir until sauce is just slightly thickened. Stir lemon juice into the sauce and remove from heat.

SWEET & SOUR DIPPING SAUCE

Makes about 3/4 cup

Apricots bring added sweetness to this tangy blend.

1/4 cup pineapple preserves (see Note)
1/4 cup apricot preserves
2 tablespoons light corn syrup
5 teaspoons white vinegar
1/2 teaspoon soy sauce
1/2 teaspoon dry mustard
1/4 teaspoon salt
1/8 teaspoon garlic powder
2 teaspoons cornstarch
2 tablespoons water

In a food processor or blender, combine and purée the preserves, corn syrup, vinegar, soy sauce, dry mustard, salt, and garlic powder.

Transfer mixture to a small saucepan and cook over medium heat until reaching a boil.

Mix water into cornstarch and stir cornstarch paste into dipping sauce. Return to a simmer and continue to stir until sauce thickens. Remove from heat. Once cooled, sauce should be stored in a covered container in the refrigerator.

NOTE: You can substitute 1/2 cup apricot pineapple jam in place of preserves.

COLD SWEET AND SOUR SOUP

Makes about 6 cups

*Put a spin on that traditional cold soup, gazpacho,
with these fresh island flavors.*

1 tablespoon olive oil
1 cup chopped Maui or red onion
2 cups chopped cabbage
6 ounces V-8® juice cocktail
2 cups water
1/3 cup fresh lemon juice
1/4 cup honey
Salt and pepper to taste
1/3 cup pineapple juice

Heat oil and sauté onions over low heat until translucent and carmelized. Add cabbage and sauté for about 5 additional minutes until completely limp. Stir in tomatoes, water, lemon juice, and honey and simmer for 15 to 20 minutes. Season with salt and pepper and remove from heat.

Cool soup and then pour into a blender or food processor and purée to a smooth consistency. Refrigerate overnight. Just before serving, mix in pineapple juice.

SOOO SIMPLE SWEET AND SOUR CHICKEN

Serves 6

Prepared soup mix and a minimum of other ingredients make this dish as easy as can be.

Pineapple Marinade (see recipe below)
2 pounds boneless, skinless chicken tenderloin fillets

Garnish: Chopped Roma tomatoes

Place chicken fillets in a glass baking dish. Pour sauce over chicken, making sure that all pieces are coated. Cover casserole and marinate chicken in the refrigerator overnight.

Preheat oven to 325 degrees Fahrenheit.

Bake for 1 hour. Serve with a sprinkle of freshly chopped tomatoes on top.

PINEAPPLE MARINADE

Makes about 1-1/2 cups

1 (1-ounce) package French onion soup mix
1/2 cup pineapple preserves (or apricot pineapple preserves)
1 cup French, Russian, or Catalina salad dressing

In a small bowl, stir together soup mix, pineapple preserves, and salad dressing. Refrigerate until used.

SWEET AND SOUR CHICKEN KEBABS

Serves 4

High heat accentuates pineapple's natural sweetness and tames any acidic bite; plus, the color adds a touch of gold to your kebabs.

Sweet and Sour Sauce (see Note)
1 (20-ounce) can pineapple chunks
4 skinless, boneless chicken thighs
2 medium green bell pepper
1 onion, cut in 1-inch chunks
8 skewers

Preheat oven to 425 degrees Farenheit. Spray a baking pan with vegetable oil spray.

Over a small bowl, drain pineapple and reserve juice. Rinse chicken and pat dry; cut into 1-inch stew-cut cubes. Place chicken in reserved pineapple juice.

Core and seed bell peppers and cut into 2-inch squares.

To create kebabs, alternate chicken, green pepper, onion and pineapple on skewers; then brush each kebab with Sweet and Sour Sauce (see note).

Place in a baking pan and bake for 10 to 12 minutes, or until sizzling hot.

NOTE: Use prepared Sweet and Sour Sauce recipes found on pages 56 to 58 or purchase already prepared Sweet and Sour Sauce.

SWEET AND SOUR 'AHI TUNA

Serves 4

*The fish here plays an almost secondary role
to an intriguing mix of papaya and pineapple with
mushrooms, bean sprouts and bell peppers.*

Sweet and Sour Citrus Sauce (see recipe on page 65)
4 (6-ounce) 'ahi (yellowfin) tuna fillets
Salt and freshly ground pepper to taste
1 tablespoon canola oil
1 cup diced red bell pepper
1 cup diced green bell pepper
1 cup rinsed and sliced shiitake mushrooms
1 cup sliced button mushrooms
1 cup mung bean sprouts
2 cups diced fresh pineapple
1 cup stew-cut papaya

**Garnish: 1/2 cup green onion tops and a sprinkle of black
sesame seeds**

Rinse fish fillet and pat dry with paper towels.

Heat a large, dry cast-iron skillet over high heat. Brush fillets lightly with canola oil and season fish with salt and pepper. Cook about 3 minutes. Using a large spatula, turn and cook other side until desired doneness, about 3 to 4 minutes for rare. Remove to a plate.

Add bell peppers, mushrooms, and bean sprouts to the skillet and stir-fry for about 15 seconds. Add pineapple and papaya and stir-fry for an additional 30 seconds. Pour Sweet and Sour Citrus Sauce into the skillet and toss until all vegetables are evenly coated.

To Serve: Plate fish and ladle sweet and sour vegetable mixture over fillet. Garnish with green onion and black sesame seeds.

SWEET AND SOUR CITRUS SAUCE

Makes about 1 cup

Ketchup and orange juice? You'll be surprised by the flavor you get from this simple blend.

1 cup orange juice

1/4 cup cider vinegar

1 1-inch piece fresh ginger, peeled and minced

1/2 cup ketchup

1 tablespoon cornstarch, dissolved in 1/4 cup cold water

In a medium saucepan, combine the orange juice, water, vinegar and ginger. Simmer for 5 minutes and add ketchup and cornstarch mixture. Stir over medium heat until sauce is thickened, about 3 minutes. Set aside.

SWEET AND SOUR TOFU STIR-FRY

Makes 4 servings

Tofu, with its mild taste and gentle texture, is a lovely canvas for a balanced sweet-sour sauce.

20 ounces firm or extra firm regular tofu

4 cups frozen Asian stir-fry vegetables (see Note)

1/2 cup pineapple juice

1 tablespoon dark brown sugar

1/4 cup apple juice concentrate

1 tablespoon rice vinegar

1 tablespoon cornstarch mixed with 2 tablespoons water to thicken

2 tablespoons peanut oil (or canola oil)

1 tablespoon finely chopped and peeled ginger root

2 tablespoons peeled and minced garlic

1 Hawaiian chili pepper, seeded and minced

2 Roma tomatoes, diced

1 cup canned straw mushrooms, drained

Salt and freshly ground pepper to taste

Cut tofu into 1/2-inch slices and set aside.

In a small bowl, combine pineapple juice, brown sugar, apple juice and rice vinegar. Set aside.

Heat peanut or canola oil in a wok or heavy skillet and add ginger, garlic, and chili pepper. Stir-fry for about 1 minute. Add frozen vegetables and stir-fry for 3 minutes more.

Add the tofu, tomato, and mushrooms and add cornstarch mixture if necessary to thicken. Season to taste with salt and pepper. Turn onto a platter and serve.

NOTE: Oriental vegetable mixes are always colorful and contain many flavors and textures. Mixes include varying combinations of bamboo shoots, bell peppers, broccoli, carrots, baby corn cobs, leeks, mushrooms, onions, and water chestnuts.

Contract laborers load fresh-picked pineapples onto a horse-driven cart. Before technological advances streamlined productivity, planting, picking and transporting pineapples were rigorous tasks done entirely by hand.

SWEET AND SOUR SHRIMP

Serves 4

The colorful mix of fresh, golden pineapple and green beans
makes this a tempting stir-fry.

1 pound fresh or frozen peeled and deveined shrimp

1 cup teriyaki sauce

1/3 cup pineapple juice

1 tablespoon rice vinegar

1/4 teaspoon hot sauce

1/4 teaspoon cornstarch

2 teaspoons canola oil

1 teaspoon peeled and minced fresh ginger

1 cup fresh pineapple chunks

2 tablespoons minced green onion

2 cups (1-1/2-inch pieces) long beans or fresh young green
beans

Garnish: Sprinkle of toasted sesame seed

Whisk together teriyaki sauce, pineapple juice, vinegar, and hot sauce. Mix into cornstarch and set aside.

In a saucepan, heat oil and sauté ginger. Add pineapple chunks and green onion and heat until pineapple begins to brown. Stir occasionally. Add teriyaki-pineapple mixture and long beans. Simmer for about 5 minutes.

In a separate heavy skillet or wok, heat oil and sauté shrimp until they just turn pink. Add to sauce and remove from heat.

Serve over a bed of rice and garnish with toasted sesame seeds.

SWEET AND SOUR PORK

Serves 4

*This standard Chinese restaurant dish
is easy to reproduce at home.*

1 pound pork tenderloin
1 tablespoon cornstarch
2 teaspoons canola oil, divided use
1 small thumb fresh ginger - thinly sliced
1 cup chopped green bell pepper
2 tablespoons white vinegar
1 tablespoon soy sauce
2 tablespoons tomato paste
1 (20-ounce) can pineapple chunks in heavy syrup

Cut tenderloin into bite-size pieces and toss with cornstarch.

In a wok or heavy skillet, heat 1 teaspoon canola oil to high and fry meat until golden brown. Remove meat and set aside.

Add oil, ginger slices and bell pepper to wok. Stir in drained pineapple syrup, vinegar, soy sauce, and tomato paste. Heat to a simmer.

Add back meat and pineapple chunks and stir well; simmer until sauce is reduced.

SWEET AND SOUR MEATBALLS

Serves 4

A sauce of soy-ginger Asian flavors and a full measure of pineapple chunks elevate this ordinary dish of meatballs.

Sweet and Sour Meatball Sauce (see recipe on page 72)
1 pound lean ground beef
1 large egg
1/2 cup dry bread crumbs
1/4 cup finely chopped onion
1 teaspoon granulated sugar
1/4 teaspoon ground ginger
1/4 teaspoon salt
1/4 teaspoon ground black pepper
1 teaspoon Worcestershire sauce
1 large carrot, diagonally sliced
1 large green bell pepper, seeded and cut into 1/2-inch
  pieces

Preheat oven to 400 degrees Fahrenheit and lightly spray a large baking sheet with vegetable oil.

In a large bowl, thoroughly mix beef, egg, bread crumbs and onion. Create a well in the meat mixture center and combine sugar, ginger, salt, pepper, and Worcestershire sauce; thoroughly mix into meatball mixture. Shape into 1-inch balls and place a single layer on a baking sheet. Bake for 10 to 15 minutes.

Add pineapple chunks, carrot, green pepper and meatballs into the sauce; gently stir to evenly coat. Simmer uncovered until meatballs are thoroughly cooked (about 20 minutes).

SWEET AND SOUR MEATBALL SAUCE

Makes about 2 cups

1 (20-ounce) can pineapple chunks in heavy syrup
2/3 cup water (divided use)
3 tablespoons distilled white vinegar
1 tablespoon soy sauce
1/2 cup packed brown sugar
3 tablespoons cornstarch
1/2 teaspoon ground ginger
1/2 teaspoon salt

Drain pineapple and reserve syrup. Mix pineapple syrup with enough water to make 1 cup; add to a large sauce pan. Stir in vinegar, soy sauce, and brown sugar and bring to a simmer.

In a separate cup, mix together cornstarch, ginger and salt. Mix water into cornstarch mixture and add to sauce. Stir until smooth. Cover and cook over medium heat until thickened.

SIMPLY SAVORY

IN THE DAYS BEFORE GREAT CHEFS INTRODUCED THE IDEA OF A HAWAI'I REGIONAL CUISINE, A SLAB O' HAM WITH A SLICE O' PINEAPPLE WAS "HAWAIIAN HAM" ON RESTAURANT TABLES. WE'VE COME A LONG WAY; THE MAIN DISHES THAT ENCOMPASS PINEAPPLE SHOW JUST HOW FAR. COMBINE THE FRUIT WITH GARLIC AND PORK CHOPS, WITH RAISINS IN POT ROAST, WITH SESAME SEEDS AND CHICKEN—THE POSSIBILITIES ASTOUND.

Previous page: In the days before mechanical assembly lines, pineapple plantation workers boxed the fruit by hand before it was transported to the canneries to be processed.

SESAME CHICKEN IN PINEAPPLE SAUCE

Serves 4

Nutty oils heated up in a wok lend depth of flavor to ordinary chicken breasts.

4 skinless, boneless chicken breasts

1 teaspoon toasted sesame oil

1 teaspoon peanut oil

2 cups crushed pineapple

2 cups chicken stock or canned low-sodium chicken broth

1 tablespoon brandy

1 teaspoon soy sauce

1 tablespoon cornstarch

2 tablespoons water

Garnish: Toasted sesame seeds

Rinse chicken and pat dry. Heat sesame and peanut oils in a heavy skillet or wok and sear chicken on both sides until brown. Add pineapple, chicken stock, brandy, and soy sauce and heat to simmering.

Mix together cornstarch and water and combine with chicken to create the sauce. Heat for 3 more minutes, stirring constantly.

Transfer to a serving bowl and sprinkle with toasted sesame seeds.

CRUNCHY PINEAPPLE CHICKEN

Serves 4

*Peanuts, water chestnuts and just crisp-tender peas
put the crunch in this dish.*

4 skinless, boneless chicken breasts or thighs
I medium onion
4 stalks celery
I tablespoon peanut oil
I (5-ounce) can water chestnuts, drained
I red bell pepper, sliced into strips
I tablespoon cornstarch
2 tablespoons water
I tablespoon soy sauce
1/4 cup fresh or frozen snow peas
I cup crushed pineapple in syrup
1/4 cup chopped peanuts
Salt to taste

Rinse and pat dry chicken breasts and slice into 1/2-inch thick strips. Set aside.

Rough-chop onion and celery. Set aside.

In a skillet or wok, heat canola oil and add chicken. Sauté chicken until just pink and transfer chicken to a plate.

Add onion, celery, water chestnuts, and bell pepper to the skillet and sauté until onion becomes translucent.

Meanwhile, mix water and soy sauce into cornstarch to make a slurry. Add to vegetable mixture, along with pineapple, syrup, and peanuts and stir for 2 minutes, or until sauce becomes thick.

Add chicken and cook for 1 more minute only.

Serve immediately over white or brown rice.

CURRIED PINEAPPLE-MANGO CHICKEN

Serves 4

Elements such as raisins, mango chutney and pineapple would normally be served as condiments to top a curry dish; here, they're cooked along with the chicken and spices.

3 skinless, boneless chicken breasts

4 teaspoons sunflower oil, divided use

I cup sliced onion

2 tablespoons peeled and minced ginger

2 tablespoons curry powder

I teaspoon cinnamon

1/3 cup raisins

3 tablespoons mango chutney

1/2 cup orange juice

2 cups fresh pineapple chunks

Salt and pepper to taste

Slice chicken into 1/2-inch thick strips and place in a small bowl. Toss with 2 teaspoons sunflower oil.

Heat skillet to hot and sear chicken for about 30 to 45 seconds on each side (until pink is just gone). Remove to a plate.

Add remaining oil and sauté onions and ginger together over medium heat until onions are translucent and caramelized. Remove to a plate.

Add curry powder, cinnamon, raisins, and mango chutney and heat until it just reaches a boil.

Return chicken to sauce, stir and cover for about 2 minutes.

Serve over rice or a grain dish like barley.

PINEAPPLE-HONEY MUSTARD-GLAZED PORK CHOPS

Serves 4

If you'd like to spice up a pork chop without the flame of chilies, try a mustard glaze for a sweet-smooth bit of heat.

3 tablespoons pineapple preserves

3 tablespoons honey mustard

3 tablespoons water

1 teaspoon Worcestershire sauce

4 (4-ounce) boneless pork loin chops (3/4-inch thick)

1/8 teaspoon kosher salt

1/8 teaspoon black pepper

Garnish: Sprinkle of chopped macadamia nuts and fresh chopped parsley

In a small bowl, mix together pineapple preserves, honey mustard, water and Worcestershire sauce.

Season chops with salt and pepper and brown chops on both sides over medium-high heat.

Add pineapple mixture to the skillet and reduce heat to low. Cover and simmer for about 5 minutes.

Garnish with macadamia nuts and parsley. Serve.

HOT AND SPICY PINEAPPLE PORK

Serves 4

Classic Chinese sweet-sour pork
picks up the heat of chili peppers.

1 pound pork loin

2 tablespoons soy sauce

1-1/2 tablespoons peeled and minced fresh ginger

1 teaspoon peeled and minced garlic

2 teaspoons canola oil

2 tablespoons chicken broth or canned low-sodium chicken
   broth

1-1/4 cups cider vinegar

3 tablespoons packed brown sugar

2 tablespoons cornstarch

1 teaspoon minced hot chili pepper

2 celery stalks, crescent-sliced

1-1/4 cups diced pineapple in heavy syrup

1/4 cup pineapple juice

1/4 cup diced cashews or walnuts

Slice pork and place in a flat-bottomed casserole. Combine soy sauce, ginger and garlic and pour over pork slices. Cover and marinate pork, refrigerated, for an hour.

In a wok or skillet, heat canola oil to hot and stir-fry pork until browned. Transfer pork to a plate.

Combine broth, vinegar, brown sugar, and cornstarch and chili pepper. Add to wok and stir constantly while simmering. When sauce begins to thicken, add celery, pineapple, and pineapple juice. Once sauce begins to boil, reduce heat and simmer for about 5 minutes. Add pork and chopped nuts and heat a few more minutes.

Serve over rice or couscous.

SLOW-COOKING PEPPER PINEAPPLE TURKEY STEW

Serves 4

A mix of vegetables, plus pineapple, simmered together to make a colorful stew, sweetened with brown sugar.

2 cups cooked turkey (see Note)

2 large carrots

2 stalks celery

1 large onion

2 large green bell peppers

1 teaspoon canola oil

2 cups water

1 cup pineapple chunks in juice

1 tablespoon packed brown sugar

2 tablespoons soy sauce

Garnish: Fresh chopped Roma tomatoes

Slice turkey into stew-size pieces. Set aside.

Clean carrots, celery, and onion and cut into stew-size pieces. Meanwhile, remove ribs and seeds from bell peppers and cut into 1-1/2 inch strips.

In a large heavy-bottomed pot, add oil, turkey, and vegetables and sauté until brown. Add water to the pot and bring to a simmer until vegetables are nearly cooked.

Stir in pineapple chunks, brown sugar, and soy sauce and heat until it reaches a simmer.

Serve over rice with the sprinkle of fresh chopped tomato.

NOTE: To use uncooked turkey, rinse and cut into 1-inch cubes. In a large heavy-bottomed pot, heat 2 teaspoons of canola oil to hot and brown turkey. Turn heat off and cover.

GRILLED PINEAPPLE-GLAZED BEEF SHORT RIBS

Serves 4

*Short ribs are a fabulous match for pineapple.
The fruit helps tenderize, while also providing
a tangy-sweet glaze.*

2 pounds well-trimmed beef short ribs, about 1/2-inch thick
1/2 teaspoon kosher salt
1/4 teaspoon ground black pepper
1/4 cup water
1 cup pineapple preserves
2 tablespoons packed brown sugar
3/4 cup chili sauce
1/4 cup cider vinegar
1/3 cup pineapple juice

Season ribs with salt and pepper and place in a Dutch oven with water. Cover and simmer until meat is tender (about 2 hours). If necessary during cooking, add more water. Drain.

Mix together pineapple preserves, brown sugar, chili sauce, vinegar, and pineapple juice.

Prepare grill or preheat broiler.

Brush beef ribs with pineapple glaze, covering them thoroughly. Grill or broil ribs for 10 minutes. Baste ribs with remaining marinade while cooking and cook an additional 4 to 5 minutes. Heat remaining sauce and serve with ribs (see note).

NOTE: Ribs may be cooked in a covered pan in a 350-degree Fahrenheit oven for 1-1/2 hours.

BEEF KEBABS WITH A TROPICAL FLAIR

Serves 4

Pineapple, cherry tomatoes, and bell peppers
bring a rainbow of color to your kebabs.

1 pound boneless top sirloin beef

1/4 cup canned pineapple juice

2 tablespoons distilled white vinegar

1 tablespoon molasses

1 teaspoon salt

1/8 teaspoon ground black pepper

1 large Maui or Ewa onion, cut into 1-inch slices

12 fresh or canned pineapple chunks

8 (1-inch diameter) firm, ripe cherry tomatoes

2 medium-size green bell peppers, seeded, ribbed and cut
   into 1-inch strips

Cut beef into 1-inch cubes. Set aside.

In a large bowl, stir together pineapple juice, vinegar, molasses, salt and pepper until well combined. Add beef cubes, cover and refrigerate for at least 4 hours, turning the beef over occasionally.

One hour prior to grilling, light a layer of coals in a charcoal broiler and let them burn until a white ash appears on the surface.

Reserving marinade, remove beef and thread cubes on skewers. Thread onions, tomatoes, pineapple and green bell peppers alternately on separate skewers from meat.

Dip meat skewers into marinade and grill 4 inches from direct heat for about 10 minutes. When meat is nearly cooked, grill pineapple and vegetables over hot coals for 5 minutes.

These kebabs are great when served with a simple tossed salad.

PINEAPPLE RAISIN POT ROAST

Serves 6

Slow-cooking with low heat deepens this dish's intriguing mix of flavors—cumin, garlic, tomato, balsamic vinegar, olives and pineapple.

1 (3-pound) blade-cut chuck roast

2 teaspoons kosher salt

2 teaspoons ground cumin

2 teaspoons canola oil

2 cups chopped white onion

6 peeled and minced garlic cloves

1/2 cup tomato sauce

1/3 cup balsamic vinegar

1 (15-ounce) sliced black olives

1 cup raisins

1 cup crushed pineapple in heavy syrup

Preheat oven to 190 to 200 degrees Fahrenheit.

Dry-rub both sides of meat with salt and cumin. Set aside.

Heat a heavy skillet (not non-stick pan) on high heat until very hot. Brown meat on both sides and remove from pan.

Lower heat and add canola oil to skillet. Heat onions until translucent and add garlic. Stir for about 30 seconds. Add tomato sauce, vinegar, olives, raisins and crushed pineapple with syrup.

Bring to a boil and simmer until the liquid is reduced by half.

In an oven casserole with lid, place roast and other ingredients and cook until the meat is tender (about 3 hours). Remove from oven and hold meat for at least 1/2 hour before serving.

HONEY LAMB KEBABS

Serves 4

*Honey and lemon, with a mix of Asian flavors,
come together in the marinade for these kebabs.*

3-pound leg of lamb
4 thin slices ginger
4 garlic cloves, crushed
3 tablespoons soy sauce
1 cup finely sliced onion
Juice from 1/2 lemon
3 tablespoons honey
Sprinkle of kosher salt
Sprinkle of freshly ground pepper
1 medium green bell pepper
3 cups fresh pineapple chunks

Remove lamb meat from bone and slice lengthwise into 1-inch strips and then 1-inch cubes.

Combine ginger, garlic, soy sauce, onion, lemon juice and honey. Season with salt and pepper. Place meat in marinade, cover, and refrigerate overnight. Boil remaining used marinade before brushing on cooked lamb.

Preheat broiler.

Thread lamb on skewers and lay on tray; broil for about 5 minutes on each side.

Meanwhile, remove ribs and seeds from bell pepper and cut into 1-1/2-inch strips.

Thread alternating pieces of pineapple chunks and bell pepper on skewers. Place on a tray and broil for about 2 minutes on each side.

For a real flair, slip kebabs off skewers and toss together in a hollowed pineapple shell.

SIMPLY SALMON AND PINEAPPLE PAPAYA SALSA

Serves 4

A simple, broiled salmon fillet, topped with a fresh, fruity salsa.

Pineapple Papaya Salsa (see recipe below)
4 (6-ounce) salmon fillets (about 3/4-inch thick)
Light sprinkle of kosher salt and freshly ground black
pepper

Preheat broiler.

Place salmon on a metal baking sheet and sprinkle with kosher salt and freshly ground black pepper. Broil fish until it just starts to firm and is no longer translucent (about 5 minutes). Turn fillets and broil about 1 more minute.

Transfer to plates and top with Pineapple Papaya Salsa.

PINEAPPLE PAPAYA SALSA

Makes 2 cups

1/2 cup diced fresh pineapple
1/2 cup diced papaya
1/4 cup minced green bell pepper
2 tablespoons fresh lemon juice
1/4 cup diced red or mild white onion
1/2 cup firm ripe tomato
1 teaspoon chopped parsley
1 teaspoon red pepper flakes
1/2 teaspoon kosher salt
1/8 teaspoon coarse black pepper

Clean fruit and vegetables. Dice and gently toss together in a medium mixing bowl. Season with lemon juice, salt and pepper. Cover and refrigerate until chilled to allow flavors to blend.

CASHEW TOFU

Serves 4

Nuts and water chestnuts add contrast to the soft edge of tofu, while pineapple and chili add depth of flavor.

1 (20-ounce) block firm tofu

1 bunch green onion (about 8 stalks)

1 tablespoon canola oil

2 peeled and minced garlic cloves

2 tablespoons oyster sauce

1 (5-ounce) can sliced water chestnuts, drained

1/2 cup crushed pineapple in heavy syrup

1 teaspoon red chili pepper flakes

1/2 cup chopped unsalted roasted cashew nuts, divided use

Garnish: Chopped cashew nuts

Freeze tofu overnight. While still slightly frozen, slice into 1-inch cubes. Set aside.

Trim green onion tops to 2-inch lengths. Set aside.

In a wok, heat canola oil and stir-fry garlic briefly until light brown. Add tofu and oyster sauce; then stir-fry for 3 minutes. Stir in water chestnuts, green onion, crushed pineapple, red chili pepper flakes and 1/3 cup roasted cashew nuts. Lightly toss until green onion tops are limp.

Chop remaining cashew nuts and sprinkle over tofu dish.

This dish goes great with brown rice.

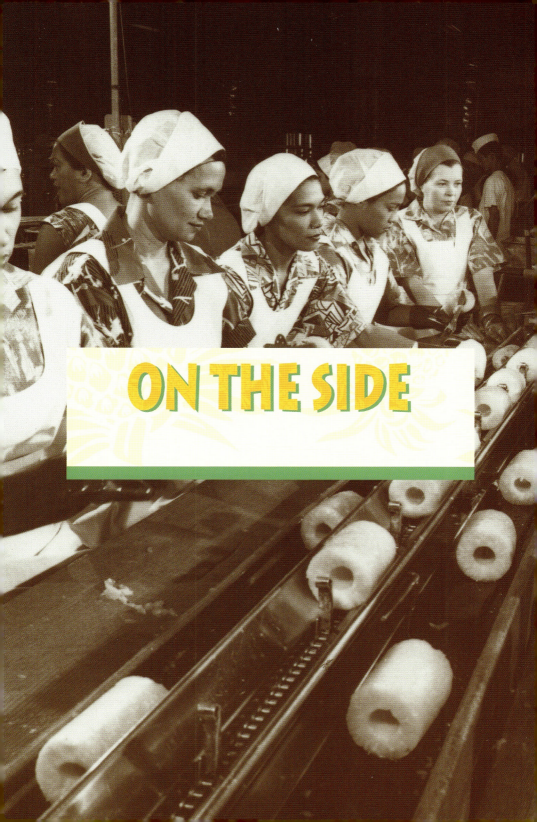

ON THE SIDE

PINEAPPLE-INFUSED
ACCOMPANIMENTS GO A LONG WAY
TOWARD PERKING UP ORDINARY ENTRÉES.
THEY ADD A TASTE OF THE TROPICS TO A
STAID THANKSGIVING TABLE, PUNCH UP
WEEKNIGHT DINNERS, ADD AN
INTERNATIONAL FLAVOR TO PICNICS AND
BARBECUES. A NUTRITIONAL SIDE BENEFIT:
COMBINED WITH POTATOES OR RICE,
THEY SNEAK A BIT OF FRUIT INTO
A MEAT-AND-STARCH DIET.

Previous page: Trimmers inspect the cored pineapples on the
conveyer belt to make sure that every bit of peel has been removed.
Next, the pineapples are sent to be sliced, sorted and canned.

PINEAPPLE-CRANBERRY RELISH

Makes about 5 cups

*Buy cranberries in the fall when they're cheap
and plentiful, then freeze this relish for a spur-of-the-moment
burst of flavor any time of the year.*

1 pound cranberries

2 apples

1-1/2 cups granulated sugar

Juice of 1 lemon

1 (20-ounce) can crushed pineapple

2 ounces brandy or Grand Marnier (see Note)

Chop cranberries and core apples with skin or briefly pulse-chop cranberries in food processor and manually chop apples. Pour into a glass mixing bowl.

Immediately toss with lemon juice to prevent apples from browning. Then add sugar, crushed pineapple and brandy and stir well.

Cover and refrigerate for at least several hours, or overnight. This relish may be frozen for spur-of-the-moment bursts of flavor anytime of the year.

NOTE: Frozen orange juice concentrate can be substituted for alcohol.

WHIPPED PINEAPPLE YAMS

Makes 4 cups

This savory twist on a Thanksgiving staple
would be a hearty side.

2 pounds yams, cut into 1-inch slices
1 teaspoon salt
Water for boiling
1/2 cup packed brown sugar
1 cup buttermilk
1/2 cup coconut milk
1 (20-ounce) can crushed pineapple in syrup

In a medium saucepan, place yams, enough water to cover, and salt. Bring water to a boil over high heat and reduce heat to a simmer until yams are soft and can be easily pierced with a fork.

Drain, cool, and peel.

In a blender or food processor, purée together yams, buttermilk, coconut milk, brown sugar, and crushed pineapple.

Place in a glass casserole and bake at 350 degrees Farenheit to rewarm or microwave for about 10 minutes.

PINEAPPLE PECAN STUFFING

Makes 4 cups

Stuffing can be mushy and boring, but fruit and nuts create interest both textural and flavorful.

2 tablespoons butter

1/2 cup chopped onion

1 cup minced celery

1 cup chopped pecans

1/4 cup finely chopped fresh parsley

1 teaspoon kosher salt

1/4 teaspoon white pepper

4 cups bread crumbs

1-1/2 cups vegetable or chicken stock

1 cup crushed pineapple in heavy syrup

Heat butter in a frying pan and sauté onion, celery, and pecans over moderate heat until onion becomes translucent.

Stir parsley, salt and pepper.

Add bread crumbs and mix well.

Pour stock into a large glass bowl and microwave for 2 minutes. Pour into stuffing mixture and stir well to moisten.

Spoon stuffing into a 3-quart casserole with lid. Cover and microwave until heated through (about 10 minutes). Let stand, covered for 5 additional minutes.

PINEAPPLE-MINT TABBOULEH

Makes about 7 cups

Tabbouleh, a refreshing salad mix, takes bulgur wheat as its base and packs it with tomatoes, cucumber, onions, parsley and mint.

1 cup medium-grain bulgur wheat

2 cups boiling water

2 cups chopped fresh tomatoes

1 cucumber, peeled, seeded, and diced

1/2 cup chopped red onion

1 bunch green onion, whites and greens, minced

1 cup fresh chopped pineapple

Grated lemon zest of 1 lemon

2 to 4 tablespoons fresh lemon juice, or to taste

2 tablespoons virgin olive oil

1/4 cup finely chopped fresh mint leaves

1/4 cup finely chopped fresh parsley

Kosher salt and freshly ground black pepper to taste

Put bulgur in a heatproof bowl and pour boiling water over bulgur wheat. Cover with a glass plate or pot lid and let rest for 1 hour.

While bulgur is soaking, prepare other ingredients and combine tomatoes, cucumber, red onion, green onion and pineapple in a separate bowl. Add lemon zest, lemon juice and olive oil. Toss to coat. Sprinkle with mint and parsley and season with kosher salt and pepper to taste.

If you can wait, chill before serving.

CROCK-POT PINEAPPLE CORNBREAD STUFFING

Makes 4 cups

A slow-cooker increases your cooking capability during busy times such as Thanksgiving, when the oven and stovetop are occupied with a turkey and all the fixings.

1 (20-ounce) can crushed pineapple in syrup
1/4 cup evaporated milk
2 cups cornbread crumbs
1/2 cup granulated sugar
1/4 cup melted butter
3 eggs, beaten
Vegetable oil spray

In a medium-size mixing bowl, combine crushed pineapple, evaporated milk, and sugar; stir until sugar is dissolved. Mix in cornbread, melted butter, and eggs.

Lightly spray the bottom and sides of a crockpot with vegetable oil spray. Pour in stuffing ingredients, cover, and cook on high for about 2-1/2 hours.

PINEAPPLE FRIED RICE

Makes about 6 cups

Don't overdo the pineapple in this dish and it will work in tandem with the sweetness of the Chinese sausage.

4 ounces Chinese sausages, cut diagonally into 1/4-inch
   slices
1/2 cup diced onion
2 tablespoons peanut oil
1 tablespoon peeled and minced garlic
2 eggs, lightly beaten
4 cups cold cooked long-grain rice
2 tablespoons soy sauce
1 tablespoon fish sauce
1 cup diced pineapple

Garnish: 1 bunch green onion, sliced into 2-inch pieces

In a large, heavy skillet or wok, heat Chinese sausages, onion and peanut oil over medium-high heat; stir-fry until onion is translucent. Stir in garlic for about 10 seconds and then stir in eggs for about 1 minute.

Decrease heat to medium. Stir in rice and sauté for 2 minutes. Mix together soy sauce, fish sauce, and pineapple and add to rice. Sauté until heated through.

In a separate small skillet, lightly sauté green onion until limp; mix half with fried rice and sprinkle the rest on top.

COCONUT THAI RICE

Makes about 4 cups

*Fragrant jasmine rice, plus creamy coconut milk,
creates exotic flavors.*

1 cup jasmine or other long-grain rice
2 teaspoons canola oil
1 cup chopped onion
3 peeled and minced garlic cloves
1 teaspoon peeled and minced ginger
1 (15-ounce) can coconut milk
1 cup crushed pineapple with liquid
3/4 cup water
1/2 teaspoon kosher salt

Rinse jasmine or long-grain rice under cold running water until water runs clear. Let drain. Set aside.

In a large saucepan, heat oil over medium heat and sauté onion and ginger until onion is translucent.

Add garlic and stir for about 30 seconds.

Stir in rice and pineapple and cover. Reduce heat to low and simmer until rice is tender and liquid is absorbed (about 20 minutes). Remove from heat and stir in coconut milk. Let stand, covered, for 5 minutes.

Sprinkle salt over rice and distribute by tossing with a fork.

CURRIED PINEAPPLE RICE

Makes about 5 cups

*Curry powder mellows the sweetness and tang
of the pineapple in this hearty accompaniment.*

1/2 cup finely chopped onion
1 teaspoon canola oil
2 peeled and minced garlic cloves
2 cups uncooked long-grain rice
1 to 2 tablespoons curry powder
2 cups vegetable broth
1 tablespoon soy sauce
1 (20-ounce) can pineapple chunks in heavy syrup
4 green onions, chopped

In a large saucepan, sauté onion in oil over medium heat until translucent; add garlic and stir. Stir in rice and curry powder, making sure the curry is evenly distributed. Add broth and soy sauce and bring to a boil. Reduce heat; cover and simmer for 20 minutes.

Remove from heat and let rice stand until liquid is absorbed (about 5 minutes).

Drain pineapple and reserve syrup for other use.

Stir in pineapple chunks and green onions.

APRICOT-PINEAPPLE COUSCOUS

Makes 4 cups

*Couscous absorbs the flavors of the ingredients
it's simmered with, in this case soaking up the fruitiness
of apricot and pineapple.*

1 cup dry couscous
1/4 cup diced dried apricots
1/4 cup diced dried pineapple
1/2 teaspoon salt
1-1/2 cups boiling water

Garnish: Freshly chopped mint

In a large lidded casserole, stir together couscous, apricots, pineapple, and salt. Pour boiling water over couscous and cover. Let rest until liquid is absorbed (about 5 minutes).

Fluff couscous with a fork and serve immediately.

TROPICAL MIXED BEANS

Makes 4 cups

Put aside the usual baked beans and try this double-bean mix for your next picnic.

1 (15-ounce) can garbanzo beans
1 (15-ounce) can kidney beans
1 red onion, chopped
4 cloves garlic, minced
2 teaspoons canola oil
1 (20-ounce) can pineapple chunks
2 tablespoons packed brown sugar
1 tablespoon fresh lime juice
2 cups seeded and chopped fresh tomatoes
1/2 teaspoon kosher salt
1/2 teaspoon black pepper

Drain beans, rinse, and drain again. Set aside.

In a large saucepan, sauté onion in canola oil until onions are translucent. Add garlic and stir for 1 minute.

Drain pineapple and add to onion, along with beans, brown sugar, and lime juice.

Stir and simmer for approximately 15 minutes. Add more water if mixture becomes too thick. Cool and then cover and refrigerate over night.

Just before serving, stir in 1-1/2 cups chopped tomatoes. Sprinkle the remaining tomato on top as a garnish.

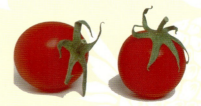

DESSERTS

SPEARS OF PINEAPPLE, ICED WELL, MAKE A LUSCIOUS DESSERT ALL BY THEMSELVES, BUT THIS FRUIT'S DISTINCTIVE SWEET-TANGY TASTE CAN ALSO BRING MUCH TO BAKED GOODS, GELATINS, PUDDINGS AND ICES.

GENERATIONS OF COOKS AROUND THE WORLD HAVE WORKED PINEAPPLE INTO THEIR AFTER-DINNER SPECIALTIES, FROM FLAN IN LATIN KITCHENS TO THE ALL-AMERICAN PINEAPPLE UPSIDE-DOWN CAKE.

PINEAPPLE IS ALSO A FAVORITE IN DESSERTS CONTAINING GELATIN, BUT IT IS IMPORTANT TO REMEMBER THAT FRESH PINEAPPLE CONTAINS SMALL AMOUNTS OF BROMELAIN, AN ENZYME THAT INHIBITS GELLING. FRESH FRUIT MUST BE BOILED 10 TO 15 MINUTES TO INACTIVATE THE ENZYME. CANNED FRUIT MAY BE USED AS IS.

Previous page: A plantation field worker lops the crowns off harvested pineapples before stacking them in crates. The crowns, along with slips and shoots from mature plants, were later planted in the soil to propagate new crops.

CANDIED PINEAPPLE AND GINGER

Makes about 2 cups

Candied fruits may be used in cookies and cakes or eaten out of hand. The Chinese often recommend ginger as soothing for a sore throat or an upset stomach.

4 thumbs fresh ginger root (about 1 cup sliced)
Water for boiling ginger and pineapple
1 cup fresh pineapple, sliced
1 cup granulated sugar
1/2 cup water for syrup
1/4 cup superfine granulated sugar (see Note)

Peel and slice ginger across the grain into thin slices. In a saucepan, cover with cold water for 5 minutes and drain. Cover again with cold water and boil for 5 minutes; drain. Spread ginger slices on clean paper towels.

In a saucepan, place pineapple slices in water and boil for 10 to 15 minutes, or until soft. Cut into bite-size candy pieces.

In a medium saucepan, combine 1 cup sugar and water and stir until sugar dissolves. Bring syrup to a boil and carefully add ginger and sliced pineapple. Lower heat and cook gently for 20 minutes, or until most of the syrup has been absorbed. Drain over a coarse sieve.

Roll ginger and pineapple (a few pieces at a time) in fine granulated sugar. Allow to dry and then store in an airtight container.

NOTE: To make superfine sugar, place 1 cup of granulated sugar in a blender and run the blender for about 1 minute.

CHOCOLATE TROPICAL FRUIT FONDUE

Makes about 2-1/2 cups

What a great idea for a party—a pot of chocolate sauce served with skewered fruit for dipping.

1 fresh pineapple

2 mangos

2 papayas

2 star fruit

2 cups Hawaiian or Portuguese sweet bread cubes

2 cups fresh whole strawberries

2 cups (12 ounces) semisweet chocolate chip

1/3 cup heavy cream or evaporated milk

2 tablespoons rum or Kirsch

2 teaspoons pure vanilla extract

Garnish: shallow bowl of shredded coconut

Prepare fruit by cutting pineapple, mangos, papayas, and bread into 1- to 1-1/2 inch cubes. Slice star fruit into bite-sized pieces. Rinse and drain whole strawberries. Place fruit and bread in separate bowls or a on large platter. Cover and refrigerate until ready to serve.

In a fondue pot or heavy saucepan, melt chocolate over low heat. In a separate saucepan add cream or evaporated milk and heat until warm. Add to melted chocolate and stir until well blended and smooth. Do not allow chocolate mixture to bubble. Stir in liquor and vanilla extract.

Place the fondue pot on its base. Light Sterno, alcohol burner or candle to keep the chocolate sauce warm.

To serve, set out small salad plates, as well as fondue forks or wooden skewers.

SLOW-BAKING CHEWY PINEAPPLE COOKIES

Makes 3 dozen cookies

You could call these "everything cookies."
They're packed with oats, applesauce, chocolate, nuts,
raisins and, of course, pineapple.

2 cups all-purpose flour
1 teaspoon baking soda
1 teaspoon salt
1 cup dry rolled oats
1/2 cup unsalted butter
1/2 cup unsweetened applesauce
2 large eggs
1 teaspoon pure vanilla extract
3/4 cup granulated sugar
3/4 cup dark brown sugar
1 cup chocolate chips
1 cup well-drained pineapple, crushed
1/2 cup crushed walnuts
3/4 cup loose raisins

Preheat oven to 300 degrees Fahrenheit and allow ingredients to reach room temperature.

In a medium mixing bowl, combine flour, baking soda, salt, and oats and set aside.

In a separate medium mixing bowl, combine butter, applesauce, eggs, and vanilla extract and beat until creamy. Add the granulated sugar and brown sugar and beat until smooth.

Gradually combine dry ingredients into butter-sugar mixture until thoroughly mixed. Stir in chocolate chips, pineapple walnuts, and raisins.

Drop rounded teaspoons of cookie dough onto an ungreased cookie sheet. Place the cookie sheet in the oven and bake for 18 to 20 minutes, or until golden brown. Remove from the oven and let the sheet stand for 2 minutes and then move cookies to wire racks to cool.

Hawaiian pineapples were trimmed to perfection by employees, then sent down the conveyor belt to be sliced and canned.

PINEAPPLE MERINGUE SURPRISE KISSES

Makes 2 dozen cookies

Pineapple pieces and chocolate chips are the surprise hidden in these light-as-air cookies.

3 large egg whites
1/8 teaspoon salt
1/8 teaspoon cream of tartar
3/4 cup granulated sugar
1/2 teaspoon pure vanilla extract
1/4 cup mini semisweet chocolate chips
2 tablespoons fresh or canned crushed pineapple (see Note)

Preheat oven to 300 degrees Fahrenheit.

Cover cookie sheet with parchment paper or a clean paper bag.

Whisk or beat egg whites until foamy. Beat in salt and cream of tartar and gradually beat in sugar (about 2 tablespoons at a time) until stiff. Fold in vanilla extract.

Using teaspoons, drop kisses onto the prepared cookie sheet. Make a small valley in the center of each cookie; place a few chocolate chips and about 1/4 teaspoon pineapple. Bake for 30 minutes and turn off oven; leave cookies in the oven for 45 to 60 minutes to dry.

NOTE: Make sure that the pineapple has been drained well to prevent soggy cookies.

PINEAPPLE CAKE

Makes 1 (9-inch) cake

*Pineapple inside and outside gives this
basic cake a taste of the tropics.*

1-1/2 cups granulated sugar

2-1/4 cups cake flour

1 tablespoon baking powder

2 large eggs

1/2 cup milk

1-1/2 teaspoons pure vanilla extract

1/2 cup crushed pineapple

Pineapple Icing (see recipe on page 117)

Preheat oven to 350 degrees Fahrenheit.

Grease and flour a 9-inch spring form pan.

In a large pan, sift together sugar, flour, baking powder; set aside.

In a small bowl, beat together eggs, milk, and vanilla extract and mix into flour mixture.

Fold in crushed pineapple and pour into a prepared baking pan.

Bake for 40 minutes, or until just done. Let cool and spread icing with a metal spatula.

PINEAPPLE ICING

Makes about 1/2 cup icing

1/4 cup crushed pineapple in heavy syrup
2 ounces cream cheese
1 tablespoon butter
1/2 teaspoon pure vanilla extract
3/4 cup powdered sugar

Bring all ingredients to room temperature.

Drain pineapple and reserve syrup from pineapple.

In a small mixing bowl, combine cream cheese, butter, vanilla extract, and powdered sugar and mix until smooth. Add pineapple heavy syrup until icing reaches the correct consistency.

Frost the cooled cake and sprinkle with drained crushed pineapple.

PINEAPPLE UPSIDE-DOWN CAKE

Makes 1 (9-inch) cake

*What's at the bottom of the pan ends up on top of your cake—
rings of pineapple beneath a brown-sugar glaze.*

3/4 cup brown sugar
1/2 cup butter, divided use
1/2 to 1 pineapple (see Note)
1 cup granulated sugar
1 egg
1-1/2 cups cake flour or 1-1/4 cups all-purpose flour
2 teaspoons baking powder
1/8 teaspoon salt
3/4 cup pineapple juice

Preheat oven to 350 degrees Fahrenheit.

In a small bowl, beat brown sugar and 2 tablespoons butter until mixture is well blended and creamy.

Spray a 9-inch cake pan with vegetable spray and press the sugar mixture against the sides and bottom of the cake pan.

Cover bottom of the pan with pineapple rings or pieces and press into the sugar mixture. Make sure that the pineapple pieces cover the bottom of the pan completely.

Combine the remaining butter and granulated sugar and beat until creamy; add the beaten eggs and blend well.

In a medium bowl, sift together the cake flour, baking powder, and salt and fold into mixture.

Add pineapple juice until mixture has the consistency to make batter.

Pour batter into the fruit-lined cake pan; bake for about 40-45 minutes then turn cake out of pan immediately to cool.

NOTE: This can be made with fresh or canned pineapple.

GRACE'S BAKED PINEAPPLE CHEESECAKE

Makes 1 (9-inch) cheesecake

*Cheesecake is by necessity rich and decadent,
but, at least in the sauce that accompanies this dish,
you get some nice, healthful fruit.*

Pineapple Sauce (see recipe on page 121)
1-1/2 cups graham cracker crumbs
1/4 cup granulated sugar
1/3 cup butter
2 (8-ounce) packages cream cheese
1 (14-ounce) can sweetened condensed milk
3 large eggs
1/4 cup fresh lemon juice

Preheat oven to 300 degrees Fahrenheit.

Bring all ingredients to room temperature.

In a medium bowl, combine crumbs, sugar and butter until ingredients are thoroughly mixed.

Press crumbs firmly on the bottom of a 9-inch spring form pan. Set aside.

Using a hand mixer, beat cream cheese until fluffy. Slowly beat in sweetened condensed milk until smooth. Mix in eggs, lemon juice, and Pineapple Sauce until completely combined.

Pour cream cheese filling into the prepared pan. Bake until the center sets (about 55 minutes). Bake until the center is set. Chill overnight.

PINEAPPLE SAUCE

Makes about 1-1/2 cups

1/4 cup granulated sugar
1-1/2 tablespoons cornstarch
1 (20-ounce) can pineapple in heavy syrup
2 tablespoons lemon juice

Place a strainer over a small bowl and drain crushed pineapple.

In a saucepan, combine syrup, cornstarch, and lemon juice and simmer for 5 minutes, stirring constantly. Add in crushed pineapple and stir until evenly distributed.

The sauce is also great served hot over ice cream or bread pudding.

PINEAPPLE CHEESECAKE WITH PINEAPPLE MANGO SAUCE

Makes 1 (9-inch) cake

*Two fabulous tropical flavors come together
in this marriage of pineapple and mango.*

Pineapple Mango Sauce (see recipe on page 123)
1-1/4 cups graham cracker crumbs
1/4 cup granulated sugar
1 teaspoon cinnamon
1/4 cup butter
4 (8-ounce) packages cream cheese, softened
1 cup granulated sugar
2 teaspoons lemon juice
1 teaspoon pure vanilla extract
4 large eggs

Preheat oven to 300 degrees Fahrenheit.

Spray a 9-inch spring form pan with non-stick vegetable oil cooking spray.

In a medium bowl, combine graham cracker crumbs, sugar, cinnamon and butter; blend well with fingertips. Press crumbs on the bottom of the prepared spring form pan.

In a large mixing bowl, beat cream cheese on low speed until smooth (about 30 seconds). Scrape the bowl after each addition. Add sugar and beat until just blended. Add lemon juice, vanilla extract, and 1 egg and beat together until just blended. Continue to add remaining eggs, one egg at a time, and beat until just blended.

Pour cheesecake filling over crust and smooth with a spatula. Bake 60 to 75 minutes (sides will be firm but center may still be slightly soft). Place the cake pan on a wire rack and cool completely. Cover and chill in the refrigerator overnight.

Once plated, pour Pineapple Mango Sauce on top. Serve.

PINEAPPLE MANGO SAUCE

Makes about 1 cup

1/2 cup crushed pineapple in heavy syrup

1/2 cup mango flesh

2 teaspoons granulated sugar

Drain and reserve syrup from pineapple.
Puree pineapple and mango in the food processor.
Heat fruit mixture over low temperature until sauce thickens.
Cool before serving.

In the 1950s, Pineapple company executives taste batches of pineapple chunks to test their sweetness and acidity.

AMBROSIA COBBLER

Serves 6

*A sprinkle of coconut finishes off this sweet mix of
pineapple and Mandarin oranges.*

Walnut Crust (see recipe on page 125)
1-1/4 cups fresh pineapple chunks
1-1/2 cups canned Mandarin oranges, drained
2 tablespoons honey
1/2 cup shredded coconut, divided use

In a medium size bowl, toss together pineapple chunks and
orange wedges. Drizzle honey on top and sprinkle with 1/3 cup
coconut. Toss again.

Spoon ambrosia filling into individual serving bowls and sprinkle
nut crust and remaining coconut on top. Top off with remaining
coconut.

WALNUT CRUST

Makes about 2 cups

1 cups all-purpose flour

1-1/2 teaspoon baking powder

1/4 cup granulated sugar

1/4 cup finely chopped walnuts

1/2 cup melted butter

1/3 cup milk

Preheat oven to 375 degrees Fahrenheit.

In a large mixing bowl, sift together flour and baking powder. Add sugar and walnuts and mix. Add butter and milk and knead together until a soft cookie dough forms.

Transfer dough onto an ungreased cookie sheet. Spread and evenly flatten dough to 1/8-inch thick. Bake until golden brown (about 10 minutes). Cool at for least 30 minutes and then crumble into small topping pieces.

PINEAPPLE RHUBARB COBBLER

Serves 6

Strawberry may be the normal match for rhubarb, but give pineapple a try for a pleasant surprise. Ginger adds the right amount of bite.

Ginger Cookie Crust (see recipe on page 127)
3 cups fresh rhubarb
1-1/2 cups pineapple chunks
1-1/4 cups granulated sugar
1/4 cup all-purpose flour
1 teaspoon cinnamon
3 tablespoons shredded coconut
2 tablespoons butter

Preheat oven to 425 degrees Fahrenheit; lightly grease a 9-inch square baking dish.

Chop rhubarb into 1/2-inch pieces and combine with pineapple in a medium-size bowl. Sift together sugar, flour, and cinnamon and sprinkle over rhubarb. Toss. Pour pineapple rhubarb mixture into the baking dish, and dot with butter. Bake about 30 minutes. Remove from oven.

Sprinkle Ginger Cookie Crust over pineapple rhubarb filling and bake an additional 20 minutes, or until crust is golden brown, at 400 degrees Farenheit.

Cool for 10 minutes and serve.

GINGER COOKIE CRUST

Makes about 2 cups

1/4 cup all-purpose flour

2 teaspoons baking powder

1 cup powdered gingersnap cookies

2 tablespoons melted butter

1/2 cup milk

Preheat oven to 375 degrees Fahrenheit.

In a large mixing bowl, combine flour, baking powder, and powdered gingersnaps. Knead in butter and milk until a stiff dough forms.

PINEAPPLE CHERRY CREAM CHEESE PIE

Makes 1 (8-inch) pie

This simple dessert is a real crowd-pleaser. Slice one up at a party and watch it disappear.

1 (8-inch) graham cracker crust (see **Note**)
1 (8-ounce) package cream cheese, softened
1 (14-ounce) can sweetened condensed milk
1/3 cup lemon juice from concentrate
1 teaspoon almond extract
2 cups crushed pineapple in heavy syrup
1 cup canned sweetened cherry pie filling

In a large bowl, whisk together softened cream cheese and sweetened condensed milk. Once blended, stir in lemon juice and almond extract.

Pour into graham cracker crust and chill overnight or until set (about 4 hours).

Place a kitchen strainer over a small bowl and drain crushed pineapple. Reserve syrup for other use.

Just before serving, carefully spoon the cherry pie filling around the outer edge of the pie. Then spoon the drained crushed pineapple into the center and spread evenly.

Serve.

NOTE: The supermarket premade molds make this dessert a cinch.

PINEAPPLE BREAD PUDDING

Makes 9 servings

Used in lieu of the usual raisins or peaches, pineapple adds weight and tartness to this bread pudding.

1 (14-ounce) can sweetened condensed milk
1-3/4 cups warm water
1 (8-ounce) can crushed pineapple in heavy syrup, undrained
1/2 cup raisins
4 cups packed crumbs of Hawaiian or Portuguese sweet bread (see Note)
3 large eggs
2 tablespoons melted butter
2 teaspoons pure vanilla extract
1/2 teaspoon salt

Preheat oven to 350 degrees Fahrenheit.

In a large bowl, stir together sweetened condensed milk, water, pineapple, and raisins.

Add bread crumbs and press down to absorb juices.

Beat eggs, butter, vanilla extract and salt together and thoroughly mix with bread mixture.

Pour into a 10-1/2 x 6-1/2-inch baking dish. Place the baking dish in a shallow pan of hot water and bake for about 45 minutes to 1 hour, or until knife inserted near center comes out clean.

Serve warm or cold. Refrigerate leftovers.

NOTE: French bread can be used if Hawaiian or Portuguese sweet bread is unavailable.

RUM GRILLED PINEAPPLE A LÁ MODE

Serves 4

Grilling caramelizes the natural sugar in pineapple and sweetens the fruit.

4 (1/2-inch) slices fresh pineapple

1/2 cup rum

2 tablespoons lime juice

2 tablespoons dark brown sugar

1 cup vanilla ice cream

Garnish: 1 teaspoon dark brown sugar

Prepare grill or hibachi for grilling (see note).

Slice pineapple and set aside.

In a bowl, combine rum, lime juice, and brown sugar. Marinate pineapple slices for about 30 minutes. Toss occasionally to ensure even coverage.

Over an open flame, grill pineapple until the fruit is tender (about 5 minutes). With a spatula, carefully transfer pineapple onto a plate and remove core. Place each hot pineapple ring into a wide-mouthed bowl and top with a dollop of vanilla ice cream.

Sprinkle with a hint of brown sugar for drama and serve immediately.

NOTE: In an oven, place pineapple on a non-stick pan and broil for 3 minutes. Turn over and broil for another 3 minutes, or until lightly browned.

PINEAPPLE HAUPIA

Makes 16 2 x 2-inch squares

*Haupia is a traditional Hawaiian dessert,
a coconut pudding that's firm enough to cut into cubes.*

1 cup crushed pineapple in heavy syrup
2 (15-ounce) cans coconut milk
1/2 cup and 2 tablespoons granulated sugar
3/4 cup cornstarch

Drain pineapple, squeeze out excess liquid and set aside.

In a saucepan, combine coconut milk, sugar, and cornstarch and stir until cornstarch in completely dissolved.

Cook over medium heat, stirring constantly to avoid lumping or burning. Once it starts to boil, reduce heat immediately to low. Once coconut milk mixture begins to thicken, stir in drained pineapple.

Stir over medium heat until thickened; pour into a shallow 8 x 8-inch pan, cover and refrigerate until set.

Cut haupia into squares and serve.

MICROWAVE TAPIOCA PUDDING WITH PINEAPPLE JAM SAUCE

Makes 2 servings

The microwave eliminates some of the mess of making tapioca, but it's the distinctive jammy sauce that makes this pudding special.

2 tablespoons granulated sugar

1-1/2 tablespoons minute tapioca

1-1/3 cups milk

1 egg, beaten

1 tablespoon pure vanilla extract

Pineapple Jam Sauce (see recipe below)

In a large glass mixing bowl, combine sugar, tapioca, milk, and egg and let stand for 5 minutes.

Cover with wax paper and microwave on high for 10 to 12 minutes, stirring every 2 minutes.

Cool for about 20 minutes and drizzle on Pineapple Jam Sauce.

PINEAPPLE JAM SAUCE

Makes about 3/4 cup

1/4 cup pineapple jam or apricot pineapple jam

1/2 cup water

1/4 teaspoon almond extract

In a glass bowl or cup, combine jam with water and microwave on high for 1 minute. Remove from the microwave and stir in extract.

PINEAPPLE TAPIOCA PUDDING WITH TOASTED COCONUT

Makes about 3 cups

Put a tropical twist on this classic dessert with pineapple and coconut.

1 (13-ounce) can coconut milk
1 cup canned crushed pineapple with juice
1 cup granulated sugar
1/4 cup quick-cooking tapioca
1 large egg, beaten
1/2 cup sweetened flaked coconut (see Note)

In a heavy-bottomed saucepan, combine coconut milk, pineapple, sugar, tapioca and beaten egg. Mix well and let sit for 5 minutes.

Cook tapioca over medium heat, stirring constantly. Once it reaches a full boil, remove from heat.

Cool for 20 minutes. Top with toasted coconut and serve warm, or cover and refrigerate and serve cold.

NOTE: To toast coconut, place flaked coconut in a small ungreased non-stick pan. Then cook over medium heat and stir constantly until lightly browned. Cool on paper towels.

PINEAPPLE GELATIN SURPRISE

Makes 8 Servings

*When using fresh pineapple in a gelatin, remember
that it must be cooked slightly first, or your dessert won't gel.
Canned pineapple may be used as is.*

1 (14-ounce) can sweetened condensed milk
1 (3-ounce) box pineapple gelatin
1/2 cup granulated sugar
2 cups boiling water
2 cups crushed pineapple (see Note)

Refrigerate the sweetened condensed milk overnight.

Next day, thoroughly dissolve sugar and gelatin in 2 cups boiling water and cool.

Beat or whisk sweetened condensed milk until stiff. Add cooled gelatin and mix well. Stir in crushed pineapple.

Pour mixture into a mold and chill to set.

NOTE: If using fresh pineapple, pare and grate pineapple and cook in 1-1/2 cups water for 10 minutes, or until tender.

PINEAPPLE MOUSSE

Makes about 4 cups

*The combination of cream and pineapple in syrup
makes this a fruity, rich dessert, but it is whisked when partly
frozen to add airiness.*

1 (20-ounce) can crushed pineapple with heavy syrup
1 teaspoon gelatin
2 tablespoons cold water
2 tablespoons lemon juice
1/2 cup granulated sugar
2 cups cream

Drain canned pineapple and reserve syrup.

Soak gelatin in cold water for 5 minutes.

Boil reserved syrup, lemon juice, and sugar for 5 minutes. Add soaked gelatin and stir until dissolved.

Strain through a piece of dampened cheesecloth; cool. Pour into a shallow pan and freeze until it begins to harden; then whisk until very light.

Beat the cream until stiff and fold it into the first mixture. Place in the coldest part of the freezer and beat the mousse with a fork once every 20 to 30 minutes.

PINEAPPLE SORBET

Makes about 2 cups

*A refreshing sorbet with the tang of pineapple is
a perfect way cleanse the palate after a heavy meal.*

2 cups water
2 cups granulated sugar
2 cups crushed pineapple in juice (see Note)
1/2 cup fresh lemon juice

Boil water and sugar together for 5 minutes. Add crushed
pineapple and lemon juice and allow to cool.

Strain through a piece of damp cheesecloth. Reserve pineapple
in the refrigerator for garnish.

Pour into a 10 x 13-inch pan and stir ice crystals at least once
an hour to create smaller, smoother ice crystals.

To serve: Scoop sorbet and top with reserved pineapple.

NOTE: Pineapple juice can be used in place of pineapple in
juice.

MEASURES AND WEIGHTS

LIQUID MEASURES

3 teaspoons = 1 tablespoon

2 tablespoons = 1 fluid ounce

4 tablespoons = 2 fluid ounces = 1/4 cup

5-1/3 tablespoons = 1/3 cup

8 tablespoons = 1/2 cup

16 tablespoons = 1 cup

1 cup = eight fluid ounces

2 cups = 1 pint

2 pints = 1 quart

4 quarts = 1 gallon

DRY WEIGHTS

1 ounce. = 28.35 grams

16 ounces = 1 pound

1 pound = 454 grams

2.2 pounds = 1 kilogram

Pineapple plantation workers take a break in the field beside a pile of freshly harvested fruit. Around 1910, field laborers worked ten hours a day—men were paid 8 cents an hour and women, 5.5 cents an hour.

SUBSTITUTIONS

'ahi (yellowfin tuna); use fresh blackfin or bluefin tuna

apple; use Asian pear

balsamic vinegar; use sherry vinegar

basmati rice; use long grain white rice

bean curd stick (dried); go to an Asian market or use thawed frozen firm tofu

butter; use margarine

buttermilk; use kefir or yogurt

Jerk spice; use Cajun spice or mixture of ground garlic, onions, chili peppers, black pepper, mustard, and celery.

Capers; use chopped green olives

cayenne pepper; use any ground hot chili pepper

Chinese cabbage; use head cabbage

cilantro (Chinese parsley); use parsley

coconut milk (thick); use 1 cup heavy cream with one teaspoon coconut flavoring

coconut milk (thin); use 1 cup whole milk beaten with 1 teaspoon coconut flavoring

cornstarch for thickening; use all-purpose flour upto 2 to 3 tablespoons flour to 1 tablespoon cornstarch

cranberries, fresh; use dried unsweetened cranberries (reconstituted)

daikon; use radish

fish sauce; use 1 part soy sauce plus four parts mashed anchovies

furikake; use ground sesame seeds and finely chopped nori seaweed sheets

garlic cloves (1); use 1 teaspoon chopped garlic or 1/8 teaspoon garlic powder

ginger (fresh grated); go to an Asian market (powdered ginger is not a good substitute)

Granny Smith apple; use any tart apple such as Gravenstein

Hawaiian sweet bread; use any sweet soft light bread

Hawaiian salt; use coarse sea salt

hoisin sauce; use pureed plum baby food mixed with soy sauce, garlic, and chili peppers

kosher salt; use coarse grain sea salt

lemon grass; use lemon zest

light olive oil; use canola oil

lup cheung (Chinese sausage); use high fat pork sausage

lychee (fresh); use canned (in water) or peeled seedless grapes

mango; use sweet ripe nectarine with a little lemon juice

Maui onion; use Bermuda, Vidalia, Ewa, red, or other sweet onion

mirin; use sweet sherry or sweet vermouth

miso; use condensed chicken broth blended with a small amount of tofu

panko; use finely ground dry bread crumbs

papaya; chrensaw melon will give similar color and texture but not the same flavor

peanuts, raw; use raw almonds or walnuts

Portugese sausage; use mild-to-hot spicy garlic-flavored pork sausage

Portugese sweet bread; use any sweet soft light bread

prawns; use shrimp

red leaf lettuce; **use any leaf lettuce**

red bell peppers; **use any bell peppers**

red chili pepper flakes; **use finely chopped seeded red chili peppers**

rice wine vinegar; **use a slightly sweetened light-colored vinegar**

scallions; **use green onions**

sesame seeds; **use finely chopped toasted almonds**

shiitake mushrooms (fresh); **use rehydrated dry shiitake or other meaty-fleshed mushroom such as portobello mushroom**

snow peas; **use sugar snap peas**

somen noodle; **use vermicelli**

soy sauce; **use 3 parts Worcestershire sauce to 1 part water**

teriyaki sauce; **use mixture of soy sauce, sake or sherry, sugar, and ginger**

wasabi (1 tablespoon prepared); **use bottled prepared horseradish with a drop of green food coloring**

wasabi (powdered); **use hot dry mustard**

watercress; **use arugula**

white pepper; **use black pepper**

won bok; **use savoy cabbage or other green cabbage**

INDEX